Samkhya Darshan

With kind regards, ॐ *and prem*

Swami Niranjan

Samkhya Darshan

Yogic Perspective on Theories of Realism

Swami Niranjanananda Saraswati

Compiled from lectures given to postgraduate students in Yoga Philosophy at Bihar Yoga Bharati

Edited by Rishi Vashishtha (Dr Peter E. Lauer)
BAPhil (Alabama), MAPhil (Georgia), PhD CompSc (Belfast)

Introduction by Swami Vigyanchaitanya
BTech (IIT, Kharagpur), MAPhil (BYB)

Yoga Publications Trust, Munger, Bihar, India

Published by Yoga Publications Trust
   First edition 2008
   Reprinted 2009

ISBN: 978-81-86336-59-5

Publisher and distributor: Yoga Publications Trust, Ganga Darshan, Munger, Bihar, India.

Website: www.biharyoga.net
   www.rikhiapeeth.net

Printed at Thomson Press (India) Limited, New Delhi, 110001

Dedication

*In humility we offer this dedication to
Swami Sivananda Saraswati, who initiated
Swami Satyananda Saraswati into the secrets of yoga.*

Contents

Introduction to Samkhya

The Rishis have propounded all the philosophical traditions of India from ancient times. They realized the spiritual truths within themselves, without the need for any external, textual knowledge. They tapped the infinite reservoirs of knowledge within the dimensions of the higher mind and gave us very brief formulas, called *sutras*. We need to make an effort to understand these sutras through holistic knowledge and penetrating insight, as they are of great practical relevance today in our daily life. Kapila was one such Rishi, who was perhaps the first advocate of philosophy and psychology. This text presents a very clear understanding of the main concepts of this path breaking philosophy, called Samkhya. The attempt here is to get into the essence of this system and present an insight into what Kapila had in mind when he first formulated the system of classical Samkhya.

Origin and history

Samkhya is an important philosophy because it forms the foundation of the Indian philosophical tradition as well as the basis for the yoga tradition. If we see the history of Samkhya, we find that it has very few sources which are comprehensive. In fact, the only complete work is Ishvara Krishna's *Samkhya Karika*, on which this work is based. Samkhya is called dualistic and atheistic, however, the versions of Samkhya in the *Bhagavad Gita* and the *Bhagavad Purana*

1

are theistic. There are further versions of Samkhya in the Ayurveda treatise, *Charaka Samhita*. References to the Samkhya terms are also found in some of the upanishads, especially the *Svetasvatara Upanishad*.

Samkhya is perhaps the earliest philosophy to emerge from the vedic corpus. The *Nasadiya Sukta* of the *Rig Veda* is said to be the inspiration behind this philosophy. The concept of Purusha is there in the Vedas, but the concept of Prakriti, as the unmanifest and the womb of creation, is acknowledged to be that of Samkhya. The evolution of creation through the subtle *tanmatras*, the gross elements, *mahabhootas*, and the mobilizing and perceiving *indriyas*, as the medium to experience that creation, completes the whole picture. The concept of tanmatra as the subtle elements is specific to Samkhya.

The word samkhya is composed of two words *sam*, meaning 'correct', 'proper' and 'discriminative' and *khya*, meaning 'knowing'. So Samkhya encourages aspirants to undertake a discriminative analysis of creation and thereby realize one's true nature. In fact, it is said in one of the sutras that all other means of knowing are impure, and only direct enquiry though *vijnana*, or intuitive knowing, can bring about the knowledge of the difference between the manifest and the unmanifest, i.e. the *vyakta* and the *avyakta*. The *Pratyabhijna* of Kashmir Shaivism also refers to direct knowing or recognition. The experiences of sages prove that direct knowing is possible. Ramana Maharshi, the sage of Arunachala, arrived at the Self through a process of deep and heartfelt enquiry. That was his path and also the path for countless others.

Samkhya and the philosophical tradition

Samkhya is one of the earliest schools of Indian philosophy and the other systems have been drawn from it. Swami Vivekananda says[1], "Kapila is the father of all Hindu psychology. The ancient system that he taught is the

---

[1] The science and philosophy of religion

2

foundation of all the accepted systems of philosophy in India, which are known as *darshanas*. They all adopt his psychology, however widely they differ in other respects. Vedanta is the logical outcome of Samkhya, and pushes its conclusions still further. While its cosmology agrees with Kapila, Vedanta is not satisfied with dualism, but continues its search for the final unity, which is the goal of science and religion alike."

Samkhya is known as a dualistic philosophy as it postulates two eternal realities: *Purusha*, the witnessing consciousness, and *Prakriti*, the root cause of creation, composed of the three gunas. The process of manifestation begins with the infusion of consciousness, Purusha, into Prakriti, the unmanifest cause of creation. It is interesting to note how Samkhya arrives at the two eternal realities through a process of logical deduction and inference called proofs or *pramanas*. The Theory of Causation postulates Prakriti as the womb of creation. Purusha is logically established as the witness, the enjoyer and the consciousness. Samkhya has outlined a very systematic structure of creation, comprising a total of twenty-five tattwas or evolutes. Purusha and Prakriti constitute the transcendental level or source of evolution. The ten indriyas, manas, ahamkara and mahat, constitute the subjective field; the five tanmatras and five mahabhootas constitute the objective field. Thus evolution is on two levels the inner and the outer.

The later philosophies have further developed this concept of evolution. Advaita Vedanta advocates the philosophy of the non-dual nature of the ultimate reality and has solved the problem of the diversified nature of creation (the One ultimate, becoming many) by postulating two levels of reality: the absolute (*paramarthika*) and relative (*vyavaharika*). Kashmir Shaivism, the most systematic amongst the different tantric philosophies, has developed a total number of thirty-six evolutes or tattwas. This system includes a detailed explanation of, and additions to, the higher stages of evolution.

Sri Krishna, the divine incarnation with all the powers and attributes of the ultimate, glorifies Kapila, the founder of the Samkhya school, as a part of himself. He says, "among the siddhas, I am Kapila" (*Bhagavad Gita* 10:26). So, if an avatar mentions Kapila as Himself, why should Kapila's philosophy be called atheistic? God is not mentioned, but presumably because Kapila did not want a transcendental aspect to be introduced in a system which was purely realistic.

There has been criticism of Samkhya in this respect, and also because it is apparently a dualistic philosophy. But it can be assumed that Kapila did not want to discuss that which is beyond the grasp of the human mind, and which is strictly a matter of experience. He did not want to go beyond a realistic view. He did not want to discuss the final nature of the reality, which is essentially formless. This point is further examined at the end of this book. Although Purusha and Prakriti are mentioned as separate realities, it is repeatedly established that they work together, and Purusha forms the substratum or the base of creation. The direction of evolution given by Samkhya is clear, and this has been developed later by other philosophies.

Salient features of Samkhya

Satkaryavada, or the doctrine of pre-existent effect in the cause, is a unique contribution of Samkhya to metaphysics and physics. The word *sat* means 'existence', *karya* means 'effect', and *vada* means 'doctrine'. This doctrine states that all effects are pre-existent in the cause and the effect is the manifest cause. This establishes that nothing new is ever produced, as something cannot come out of nothing. This means that the creation never began and will never end, although there will be differences in the degrees of manifestation. It also establishes that the stage of *pralaya*, or dissolution, is the state of potentiality. In this state all the tattwas rest in the womb of Prakriti until the beginning of the next cycle of creation. This is the logical basis for the concept of eternity, which is difficult to understand, as we are faced with a constantly changing material existence.

Satkaryavada also establishes the law of conservation of energy, which is a basic principle upheld by modern physics.

Energy is converted from one form to another, but there is never any change in the primal energy. This is what Satkaryavada's ancient law of pre-existent effect in the cause tells us. This book also explains how understanding Karyakaranavada, Satkaryavada and the principles of the laws of causation can be used in modern daily life; for example, how one can get out of depression.

Samkhya also gives us a very exhaustive description of the three *gunas*, the basic material of creation. It states that all objects of the world are characterized by three properties: pleasure, *preeti*, pain, *apreeti*, and indifference, *udasin*. The same object can create these reactions in different people. This means that the basic matter of creation will also contain these three elements. Thus the deduction is that Prakriti consists of the three gunas: *sattwa, rajas* and *tamas*, which have these three properties respectively: pleasure, pain and indifference. All the objects of creation have these gunas in different proportions.

Samkhya further gives a clear picture of the human mind with its three components of *buddhi*, intelligence, *ahamkara*, ego sense, and *manas*, the deliberating faculty at the level of *indriyas*, or sensory organs. The three together (buddhi, ahamkara and manas) are called the *antahkarana*, or the inner instrument. Buddhi, or the higher mind, has the qualities of virtuous conduct based on full understanding, *dharma*; wisdom or *jnana*; non-attachment, *vairagya;* prosperity, *aishwarya* and ascertainment, *adhyavasaya*. Manas, or the lower mind, receives the sensory inputs, deliberates over them and presents the information to the higher mind, buddhi or mahat, which is the medium for Purusha (the Self). In fact, the sensory organs of knowledge are called *buddhi indriyas*. It is also mentioned that the sensory organs are not only external, but they also have corresponding internal centres.

These three components of mind form the instrument of cognition, of which are three forms: direct perception, inference and testimony. However the real cognizer is

5

Purusha, the consciousness. Buddhi (also known as mahat) is only the reflected light of Purusha; it does not have the nature of self-awareness. Thus, thousands of years ago, Samkhya established the ground for a total psychology, emphasizing that the real Self is beyond the mind.

Samkhya says the mind is a creation of Prakriti, which is also the source of all manifest creation. This implies everything in the universe is connected because all are evolutes of the same source. Man is also a product of Prakriti and must follow the laws of Mother Nature. Thus we find that the basis for modern ecology was also established by Samkhya.

Samkhya repeatedly emphasizes that the visible world is only a small portion of the totality of existence, and there is an infinite, unmanifest dimension. Logical arguments are given to validate the existence of the subtle dimension of existence. The tanmatras are the subtle elements, which cannot be seen, but their existence can be inferred; just because we cannot see it, does not mean that the world is not round. Our field of perception is limited, but we can expand our awareness through spiritual means to experience the twenty-five elements that comprise the entire existence. It is, not necessary to be bound by the material world perceived by the senses.

Samkhya and yoga

Samkhya and yoga are two parts of one system. Kapila's Samkhya is the metaphysics and Patanjali's yoga is the method or *sadhana*. Yoga follows the same philosophical system as Samkhya, viz. Purusha, (also called *drashta*, the seer) Prakriti (also called *drishya*, the seen), and the gunas. Yoga has developed the Samkhya system into the step-wise gradation of *ashtanga* yoga, or the eightfold path. The direct realization of Samkhya is replaced by an eight step climb into the higher dimensions of samadhi, and ultimately *kaivalya*, aloneness or liberation. Samkhya does not mention samadhi, but only the last stage of kaivalya. However, one does in fact come across the different evolutes of the Samkhya system like the tattwas, tanmatras, ahamkara and mahat in the stages of samadhi.

The cause of all suffering is the superimposition of Purusha, the pure consciousness, on Prakriti, the constantly changing, creative matrix. This superimposition is called *samyoga*, and this comes about because of ignorance (of the true nature of reality), or *avidya*. This ignorance is beginningless, but has an end in self-realization. It is emphasized repeatedly both in yoga and Samkhya that Prakriti has no effect for a siddha, as he or she is no longer subject to the play of the gunas having gone beyond them.

Samkhya briefly mentions the ethics of contentment, *tushti*, charity, or *daya*, and non-attachment, *vairagya*, as means on the path. Yoga evolves this idea of ethical life as the first step on the path, and gives us the five *yamas* and five *niyamas* (codes of conduct). The basic purpose of the ethical life is to take the aspirant to the dimension of sattwa, away from the pull of rajas and tamas prevalent in normal life. From Samkhya, we know that the sattwic dimension is responsible for *jnana*, or wisdom, and mahat or buddhi reflects Purusha, the consciousness, because of the predominance of sattwa. In fact, the whole of yogic life is a progression from the tamasic and rajasic aspects to the sattwic, and then transcending the gunas.

Samkhya says direct perception, inference and testimony are the three means of right knowledge (*pramana*). Yoga accepts these three, but adds four other types of knowledge: false knowledge, *viparyaya*; imaginary knowledge, *vikalpa*; past knowledge, *smriti*; and no knowledge, *nidra*. These five cover the entire field of knowledge of the ordinary mind. They are called fluctuations of consciousness, or *vrittis*, and they are caused by the beginningless ignorance. The purpose of yoga is to stop these fluctuations and thus reveal the light of Purusha, who is seated inside as the unfluctuating *drashta*, or seer.

Yoga gives the practical means for elevating our level of consciousness, and Samkhya tells us what to expect as we travel on our inward journey, by the light of sattwa through the subtle world of the tanmatras. For an aspirant on the path of yoga, the evolutionary system of Samkhya gives an explanation for some of the techniques of self-realization. For instance, it is mentioned in bhakti yoga that *bhava* and *rasa* are the qualities developed in the path of devotion, the *bhakti marga*. These qualities are concomitant with the awakening of sattwa, but we find it difficult to identify with them as we rarely experience sattwa.

Similarly, Samkhya can throw light on the guru-disciple relationship. The guru removes the ignorance of the disciple. What is the nature of this ignorance? This becomes clear through Samkhya. The level of ignorance is the last level of evolution, consisting of the gross elements and the eleven indriyas, the plane of senses and sensory objects. The guru brings the light of sattwa to the disciple and awakens his or her buddhi, or discriminative power. Thus, at every point of spiritual evolution, the knowledge of Samkhya metaphysics will broaden the understanding and provide a clear direction for the aspirant.

1

Dualism or Dvaita Vada

Samkhya is a darshana which believes in ultimate duality. Dualistic schools, including Samkhya, maintain that creation, manifestation and absorption cannot take place without a combination of two ultimate entities. Just as a sound is created when we clap two hands together, creation takes place when two forces come together. In Samkhya, these forces or principles are known as Purusha and Prakriti. There are also many *darshanas*, schools, views and theories, that are monistic in nature and say that *Brahman*, the supreme Self, or God, is the one, ultimate and only reality. The monistic *Advaita* darshana says this universe manifests from that one reality and, when the cycle of creation is complete, a cycle of absorption begins during which everything again merges back into the one supreme Self, the one supreme consciousness. The one manifests itself as many, and at the end, the many again merge into the one.

The word *Purusha* has been defined as consciousness which sees and knows, the consciousness which has knowledge but does not have the capacity to act. In Sanskrit, the definition of Purusha is: *Puri shete iti purushah*. The word *puri* means 'citadel', i.e. the body (*sharira*), and *shete* means that which is 'dormant', 'latent' or 'inactive'. So, Purusha is that which is dormant or inactive in the manifest dimension. The word *Prakriti* is derived from *pra*, a prefix denoting intensity of action, plus *kriti* meaning 'to perform', 'to do', 'to act'.

9

Prakriti denotes the primordial energy, the force of action or creation. Here we have Samkhya's two definitions of the two ultimate realities: *Purusha*, indicating consciousness, meaning the knower, the seer, the inactive witness, also known as *drashta*, and *Prakriti*, representing the force of creation, differentiation, performance and participation.

Seshvaravada and Nirishvaravada

Samkhya is known as *Dvaita Vada*, or dualistic philosophy, because it gives equal weight to both concepts: Purusha and Prakriti. However, there is another consideration. One school says, is there not a third force that brings the hands together in order to create a sound? Because the hands are part of a bigger organism, which is known as the body and mind, the *sthoola* and *sukshma* sharira, and at its instigation the hands actually come together, clap and make a sound. Another school of thought says that, although the body-mind is a bigger organism, only the hands create the sound. We may will or desire a clapping sound, but in the absence of hands, clapping cannot take place and there will be no sound.

In Samkhya, there are two schools of thought: *Nirishvaravada* and *Seshvaravada*. The word *vada* means 'discussion' or 'thought'. The word *seshvara* is derived from two roots: *sah*, meaning 'with' and *Ishvara*, 'God'. This form of Samkhya recognizes that the hands are extensions of a greater organism, and only when that wills it do the hands come together and make a sound. In other words, Seshvaravada says that Purusha and Prakriti are extensions of Ishvara, and when Ishvara wills it, these two forces come together and creation takes place. Seshvaravada means the thoughts on Samkhya which accept God, the supreme Self, as the original source.

The second main school of thought in Samkhya is Nirishvaravada. The prefix *nir* means 'without', so *Nirishvaravada* means discussions on Samkhya without reference to God or Ishvara, or with denial of the supreme Self. The premise of this branch of Samkhya is not to deny the existence of God, but it does emphasize that although God may exist, Purusha and Prakriti are the important principles. In their absence, manifestation cannot happen, just as clapping cannot take place in the absence of hands, even though the body may desire it. This theory is known as Nirishvaravada. The Samkhya that is explained in the *Bhagavad Gita* belongs to Seshvaravada. Krishna himself states, "I am the cause and the effect; everything comes from me and merges back into me. But while things are being created, each has their function to perform. Purusha and Prakriti are subsidiary to me, and each has a function to perform." However, Kapila Muni, the sage who first formulated the Samkhya philosophy, propounds Nirishvaravada. Just as the credit goes to Sage Patanjali for codifying the system of yoga in the *Yoga Sutras*, so the credit goes to Kapila for writing down the sutras which describe the Nirishvaravada philosophy of Samkhya. His Samkhya sutras became the basis for the understanding, development and expansion of the Samkhya philosophy.

Fundamental texts of Samkhya

According to tradition, Sage Kapila wrote two different treatises: *Samkhya Pravachana Sutra* and *Tattwa Samasa Pravachana Sutra*, neither of which exist now. The *Samkhya Pravachana Sutra* was the first treatise in which Kapila expounded the basic concepts of the Samkhya system. In the *Tattwa Samasa Pravachana Sutra*, he expanded on the theories, concerning the *tattwas*, or elements, and explained creation as the result of combinations and permutations of the elements. Possibly because these concepts were too complex for his time, people gave up trying to understand them after two generations.

A third generation disciple, named Ishvara Krishna, wrote the *Samkhya Karika*, which describes the entire philosophy of Samkhya as taught by Kapila, and has now become the basis of the Samkhya tradition.[1] Different commentaries have been

---

[1] See Appendix for original Sanskrit, transliteration and a modern translation of the Samkhya Karika

11

written explaining its seventy-two *slokas*, or verses. Gauda-pada, the grand-guru of Adi Shankaracharya, wrote a very famous commentary known today as the *Gaudapada Karika*, and therefore Advaita Vedanta refers to, and disputes with, Samkhya. Many Buddhist thoughts also reflect Samkhya ideology, because Buddha, before he became realized, studied Samkhya with Rishi Alar Kalam, and therefore Samkhya became a basis for Buddhist philosophy. Samkhya is also the basis for Mahavira's philosophy of Jainism, for the philosophy of Sri Krishna as taught in the *Bhagavad Gita*, and for the philosophy of yoga codified in the *Yoga Sutras* of Patanjali.

Philosophy of knowledge and numbers
There are two schools of thought regarding the significance of the word Samkhya. One school defines Samkhya, as coming from the roots *sam*, meaning balanced, equal, harmonious, and *khya*, meaning knowledge, understanding, wisdom. Here Samkhya is defined as total, perfect knowledge of the entire process of manifestation, evolution and absorption. The other school asserts that Samkhya is derived from the Sanskrit word for relating to numbers, enumeration or calculation. The spelling is the same, but the accent becomes different. The philosophy is pronounced *Saamkhya* with a long *sa*; the word relating to numbers only has a short *sa* sound. In the latter interpretation, the philosophy is called Samkhya, because its Theory of Manifestation recognizes twenty-five different stages of evolution. The description of these twenty-five tattwas or elements forms the basis of the Theory of Manifestation in Samkhya and related philosophies.

We can say the Samkhya philosophy represents both knowledge and numbers. However, Samkhya also defines what it means to be scientific. Samkhya uses the term *anvisiki* to mean 'enumeration of the contents of a particular subject matter by means of systematic reasoning'. Later the term Samkhya was used to mean a methodology of reasoning that results in spiritual knowledge (*vidya*, *jnana* or *viveka*), leading to liberation from *samsara*, the manifest world, which is subject to the three forms of suffering. In the *Samkhya Karika* of Isvara Krishna it states:

Duhkhatrayaabhighaataat jijnaasaa tadapaghaatake hetau;
Drishte saa'paarthaa chet naikaantaatyantato'bhaavaat. (1)

When one is afflicted by the three kinds of suffering *(dukhatraya)*: internal *(adhyatmika)*, external or due to nature *(adhibhautika)*, and divine or celestial *(adhidaivika)*, there arises a desire to know the means of terminating them. If it be said that this enquiry is superfluous, since ordinary remedies exist (such as medicines, etc.), it is not so, because these remedies are neither permanent *(atyanta)* nor complete *(ekanta)*.

(*Samkhya Karika,* verse 1)

Theory of Causation
The basic philosophy of Samkhya is its Theory of Causation, which is based on the theories of Karyakaranavada or Satkaryavada. The theory of cause and effect is known as *Karyakaranavada*; the word *karya* means 'effect' and *karana* 'cause'. *Satkaryavada* is the theory of the inherence of an effect in its cause prior to its manifestation; the root *sat* meaning 'existence'. Samkhya's Theory of Causation basically states that the effect is already inherent in its cause, and it is up to something else to bring out that effect. For example, clay is the material cause, an earthen pot is an effect, but there are many possibilities inherent in the clay, and each possibility represents a possible effect or manifestation. The earthen pot is an effect, a possibility that already existed in the cause before manifestation.

Wherever elements exist, they contain the possibility of transformation. Whatever the cause, it contains the inherent effects. That is the basic Theory of Causation in Samkhya. The concept of samyoga was added later. *Samyoga* means 'combination' and 'permutation'. A potter cannot make a pot from only one element but has to mix elements, such as

13

water, earth and glazes; that is where samyoga, the combination and permutation of the elements, comes into the picture. Each combination and permutation produces a different result and in Samkhya, the concept of samyoga is explained in detail in the Theory of Manifestation. But the main contribution of Samkhya to our understanding of causation is that the inherent effect is contained in the cause prior to the manifestation of that effect, and that the law of cause and effect governs the whole world. For example, a sweet taste exists in sugar. Sugar is the cause, the sweet taste is the effect, and they are linked.

2

Theory of Causation

Karyakaranavada is the theory of compatibility of cause and effect. The first argument in Samkhya is that cause and effect go hand in hand. An effect is inherent in a cause, and the cause and effect have to be compatible. Each cause has an effect, which is compatible with its cause. When we talk of cause and effect, we are assuming compatibility between the two. If two things are incompatible, then one cannot be the effect and the other its cause; rather one must be an external and independent effect, wrongly superimposed on an unrelated cause. Every effect has a cause, according to its quality, and the quality of the effect is determined by its cause. In the *Samkhya Karika* it states:

Asadakaranaadupaadaanagrahanaat sarvasambhavaabhaavaat;
Shaktasya shakyakaranaat kaaranabhaavaachcha sat kaaryam. (9)

An effect (*karya*) pre-exists or resides (*satkarya*) in its cause in a potential state or condition prior to the operation of the cause since: something cannot arise from nothing; effects require adequate material causes (*upadana*); all effects cannot arise from all causes (*sarvasambhavabhavat*); an efficient cause can only produce that for which it is efficient (*shaktasya shakyakaranat*); an effect is of the same essence as its cause.

(*Samkhya Karika*, verse 9)

15

Nimitta karana and shakti karana

The question then arises: if an effect is contained in the cause, what brings forth the effect from the cause? There has to be a catalyst or instrument. In Sanskrit, that instrumental cause is called *nimitta karana*. Its function is to bring forth the manifest effect from the cause, to give form or actuality to the possibility. Here a third concept is introduced. First is the cause, second, the effect, and third, the means or process of manifesting the effect from the cause, which is known as nimitta karana.

Another argument is that the actualization of a specific effect requires a specific cause. For example, if you wish to produce yoghurt, a specific item, you need to have milk; you cannot produce yoghurt out of water. If you wish to have cotton clothes, you need cotton, not woollen, cloth. For actualizing specific effects, you have to choose that specific cause which inherently contains the specific potential to actualize that particular effect. This choosing and empowering is involved in the concept of *shakti karana*.[2]

So in the Theory of Causation, the first argument establishes that the effect is contained in the cause, but that is a very general idea. The second argument maintains that there must be a catalyst or an instrument to bring out the effect from the cause. The third argument is that actualizing a specific effect requires a specific cause. It is the need for recognition of the cause and the relevant effects contained in the cause, which is indicated by the third argument. Another implication is that the effect is always contained in the cause, even in its unmanifest form; because it is unmanifest does not mean that the effect cannot be produced.

---

[2] It seems that the ultimate empowering shakti is the attention of consciousness – as soon as consciousness focuses on a potential cause it becomes active, becomes a process. And absolute consciousness is simultaneously aware of all causes and effects, rendering the whole of moola prakriti active. But once active, the causes develop according to their own laws. Human beings are very special 'causes' since they have reflective awareness of themselves.

Self-knowledge arising from Samkhya

We could overcome mental depression, despair and pessimism by applying this concept to our problems in life. When we are disturbed and unsure about which course of action to follow, the dilemma can be resolved by understanding the causes and effects related to the situation. Initially, the existence of the effect is not felt, because it exists in the cause in its unmanifest form. It is very difficult to realize that the cause is always there, the effect is always there, and that both can be recognized simultaneously. Often we cannot recognize the effect of a cause, or the cause of an effect, and we get involved in one without understanding the other.

We need to make an effort to discover the effect in the cause, and also the cause in the effect. For example, we may fall into depression because of something that happens during the day, such as an argument or a fight. At night, we may think about it rationally and logically, and then go to sleep without realizing that what happened has affected some deeper part of our mind. The next morning, when we get up, we feel gloomy and depressed, with no motivation to start the day. We know the external cause for the depression, but we do not know the internal part of the mind it has affected, because we have only sorted it out logically.

This means that an area of the mind has been affected, which we were unaware of, so it is necessary to find out what are the deeper causes and effects. Has the argument or fight affected my emotions? Has it given me a sense of isolation and loneliness? If so, then which feeling, belief or emotion caused this to arise? We need to know whether the emotion that caused it was affection, love, desire, rejection or aversion. There are different areas of the mind where we are not logically aware of the subtle effects of an interaction. We also need to look past the effects in order to deal with their fundamental causes. When we understand the manifestation of these elements of Samkhya, we will start to wake up and achieve deeper and more extensive self-knowledge.

17

Potent cause and desired effect

We have introduced the concept that only through a potent and selective cause, shakti karana, can the desired effect be attained. Milk is the material cause of butter, yoghurt, cheese, etc., but to obtain these specific effects of milk also requires the selection and activation of appropriate causes. Also, one cause can have many different effects. Wood, for example, can be converted into various different objects, but it will always remain wood, the different objects will conform to their common material cause. Whether you make a door, a table or a chair, the wood will always be recognized as wood, whereas milk is not recognized in butter, although butter is a product of milk.

The causes that have a single effect are determined by their *swabhava*, or natural quality. The causes that have multiple effects are recognized by their quality of containing different possibilities. Each possibility in a cause is known as a shakti karana, a potent cause. You cannot make butter out of wood, because the shakti karana for butter is absent in wood; milk is a potent cause in making butter, not wood. By studying the swabhava, and the quality, or *guna*, of the possible causes, the potent cause is recognized. Once a potent cause is recognized, you can attain the desired effect by knowing the potentialities of that cause.

Shakti karana is both singular and multiple; it represents the quality and sub-qualities which are able to manifest. For example, what is the shakti karana, or potency, contained in chalk or crayon? It cannot be eaten; for us, its primary or intended effect is writing. With milk, however, if you desire butter, then butter becomes the intended effect. If you desire yoghurt, yoghurt becomes the intended effect, and the milk is transformed into yoghurt. So when these two, the potent cause and the desired effect, are taken together, then we need the *nimitta karana*, the efficient cause, the medium to manifest or actualize the potential.

We can also explain nimitta karana by using the example of a seed. Although a seed contains shakti karana, the

18

possibility of a tree, it will not grow into a tree if you just hold it in your hand. There has to be a nimitta karana, an efficient cause or medium, by which the seed can grow. One aspect of the medium is the soil, but just putting the seed in the soil is still not enough. The seed will not sprout if you do not provide water; it will lie dormant in dry soil without germinating. A seed represents karana, the cause, for karya, the effect, but the effect cannot manifest without the efficient cause, nimitta karana, to actualize its potential.

Awareness is the key
In your life, you must consider which seed is the potent cause for your desired effect. A seed could be of any tree: apple, mango or teak. You must recognize the specific potency, the guna, or quality, which is contained in that seed. The difference in the type of karya, or effect, is the result of this quality. A seed is a seed, but if you want a mango tree, you must recognize a mango seed, and then it becomes the shakti karana for you. If you do not recognize the seed as a mango seed, but believe that it is an apple or a teak seed, then you have not discovered the natural potency of the seed. The moment you correctly identify the mango seed, you also recognize the potency which is in that seed.

When you put a seed in the ground, desiring a specific effect, the nimitta karana becomes the process of nurturing and assisting the growth of the seed by providing the right amount of water, fertilizer, etc. The nimitta karana is the medium through which you help to bring forth the potency contained in a cause. Then *utpadam*, or actualization, of the potential in the seed takes place. Here, the link between karana, or cause, and shakti karana, or potent cause, involves recognition or awareness. Your awareness, perception and knowledge must become involved for recognition of the shakti karana to take place.

The cause is not only an object; it also contains an extra potency. For the karya, or effect, to become the desired effect, this potency must be recognized through knowledge

19

and awareness, then it gives birth to the special effect that you desire. That manifestation is known as utpadam, actualization of the potential contained in the cause. The shakti karana only becomes active, when you foresee the possibility or the potentiality through your knowledge and understanding. In this process, knowledge, awareness or recognition is called *jnana shakti*, desire is called *iccha shakti* and actualization is called *kriya shakti*.

Five proclamations

These ideas about causation are summarized in the Sanskrit slokas given by Ishvara Krishna in his text *Samkhya Karika*. We can call them the five proclamations of the theory of causation:

1. If the actualization of the effect does not happen, then the cause cannot be the true source of the effect: *asadakaranat*.
2. Before manifestation, the effect is contained in the cause and it is part of the cause. In the material cause, we find the matter that is invariably contained in the effect: *upadanagrahanat*. The word *upadana* means 'matter' or 'substance' and *grahnat* means 'contained'.
3. A specific effect requires a specific cause: *sarvasambhava-bhavat*. Literally, *abhavat* means 'due to the absence of'. *Sarvasambhavat* means 'everything does not come out of everything'.
4. A desired effect can be attained only from a potent cause: *shaktasya shakya karanat*. This implies that the cause determines both the quality and quantity of an effect.
5. Cause and effect are inseparable; they are two stages of one substance. A substance in its unmanifest form is the cause, and in its manifest form, the effect: *karanabhavat*. In the existence of cause exists the effect, and they both have, so to speak, equal weight. The weight of the wood used to make a table is the same as the weight of the table that contains the wood. The weight of the earth used to make a pot is the same as the weight of the earthen pot. Both are equally potent and equally weighted.

3

Prakriti

In regard to Prakriti and the qualities of Prakriti, the first point to consider is that the entire creation is a series of effects. If you look at creation as a series of effects, then you will wonder what is the cause of these myriads of forms and myriads of effects. These effects are both gross and subtle. Gross means something that can be perceived with the senses, like trees, mountains, stones, fruits and flowers. A subtle manifestation is something that you cannot perceive externally through the senses, but which exists or subsists in the mind, such as thoughts, desires, intellect and self-identity.

There have been wide ranging discussions to discover the original or primary cause, the *moola pradhana*, to explain the manifestation of so many different effects. There are two schools of thought in Samkhya. One school says that Purusha is the cause, and the other says that Purusha cannot be the cause, because Purusha is free from cause and effect. Purusha is not the cause of any gross or subtle object, nor is Purusha an effect. Purusha is pure, static consciousness, and therefore, something else must be the primary cause, the moola pradhana.

Purusha is pure absolute knowledge, *jna*. In that pure, unadulterated state of being, where only total knowledge exists, there is no primary cause or primary effect. The cause and effect both dissolve in knowledge; therefore, Purusha cannot be the primary cause. Purusha is not an effect in the sense that it is neither gross nor subtle. It exists in the form of *akasha*, space or ether. It is vast and infinite, like the boundless space. You cannot contain space in any way, form or place, because limitation is not the nature of absolute space. Therefore, something else has to be the primary cause of this entire manifest creation.

Atomic theories of creation

Different philosophical systems have gone through a process of speculation, analysis and observation in relation to this question. Buddhism, Nyaya, Vaisheshika and Mimamsa have said that the main cause of creation is the subtle substance, known as *paramanu*, the atomic structure, which gives rise to the manifestation of earth, water, fire and air as combinations of these ultimate atoms. There are atoms and molecular structures in these four elements and therefore it was argued, many centuries ago, that the atom is the prime cause of manifestation. However, Vedanta and Mahayana, a later school of Buddhism, maintained that the primary cause of creation is consciousness, *chetana*, because consciousness controls both the gross and subtle molecular and atomic structures.

Samkhya's Theory of Manifestation

Samkhya's Theory of Manifestation is also sometimes called the Theory of Creation or the Theory of Evolution. According to Samkhya, the process of creation or manifestation has two forms, gross and subtle. The atomic theory can definitely be accepted for the existence of the gross manifestation, which is perceivable through the senses. However, you cannot explain subtle manifestations by the atomic theory; these must have another cause. You can say that consciousness is the primary cause for the manifestation of subtle states, such as different states of mind, but consciousness cannot create the molecular, atomic or subatomic particles, such as neutrons, protons and electrons, by thought alone.

Therefore, in order to understand evolution, Samkhya established this Theory of Manifestation. Samkhya brings in Prakriti as the primary cause of creation and Prakriti is defined as both insentient, *jada*, and subtle, *sukshma*. Samkhya can explain both gross manifestations, such as objects or the body, and subtle manifestations, such as the ego or thought, because of these attributes of Prakriti. By citing the concept of Prakriti as the primary cause, it is possible to explain how things in general, and body and mind in particular, came into being. This basic concept of Samkhya enables the Theory of Manifestation to be useful in a person's search for self understanding.

Attributes of Prakriti

So, Prakriti was proposed as the primary cause, or *Pradhana*, but in order to be the source and controller of both cause and effect, Prakriti must have certain special attributes. Prakriti itself is not a cause like other causes. From the primary cause, all causes come into being. All the causes and effects are inherent in the primary cause, so all the manifest objects and experiences are dependent on Prakriti, but Prakriti itself is causeless and free. Prakriti is not a cause in the usual sense; it is the mother of causes, containing all causes and their effects.

However, if the theory of potent cause is applied here, there would have to be an equally potent effect, and there is no potent effect equal to Prakriti. So, Prakriti is not a cause in itself. There are different ways of looking at potency. For example, the potency of growth in a seed will lie dormant until the right environment is provided for it, but then it will grow into a plant according to its nature; here, potent cause has an equally potent effect. But Prakriti is so potent that it does not have an equally potent effect, either qualitatively or quantitatively.

In order to understand the attributes of Prakriti as the primal cause, Samkhya gives the names, aspects and qualities of Prakriti as follows:

1. The word *Prakriti* is derived from two roots: pra plus kriti. *Kriti* denotes *kriya*, the root of action, and *pra* is a prefix, signifying intensity. Prakriti has the potency of action and is the basis of all manifestation, yet it is uncaused in itself.

2. Prakriti is *Pradhana*, the main cause. All the effects of manifestation are dependent on Prakriti, yet Prakriti is independent of all the effects.

3. Prakriti is known as *Brahma*, being a state that evolves and is responsible for evolution. Prakriti is equated with Brahma, because it evolves from jada, an insentient state, into different forms or objects, which further its progress towards realizing the existence of Purusha. Prakriti is known as Brahma, because it evolves in nature and this name validates the concept of Prakriti as a force of manifestation, growth and evolution.

4. Prakriti is known as *avyakta* or *moola prakriti*, the unmanifest, where all the causes and effects exist in a state of dormancy. Prakriti is the cause of all causes. When all causes remain in a state of dormancy, their potential effects are also dormant; they are unmanifest and imperceptible.

5. Prakriti is also known as *anumana*, inference, because the nature of Prakriti cannot be recognized or perceived directly. There is no direct knowledge of Prakriti, but you can speculate. You can infer the existence of Prakriti and her qualities by looking at various effects and considering the causes of those effects, which are themselves expressions of Prakriti. However, the causes and effects are countless, so the totality of Prakriti cannot be known. The effects are gross and subtle. Subtle effects are beyond the perception of the five senses, but the aid of inference is necessary even with gross effects.

So, Samkhya says it is impossible to know the depth and potency of Prakriti through sense-based cognition; the only way to know something of the nature of Prakriti is through anumana, inference, based on gross or subtle effects, and this is quite valid. Consider, for example, what are the causes and the effects of ego? Nobody can answer this fully. It can be inferred that this may be the cause and that may be the effect, or this may be the source and that may be the result. However, no direct sensory perception of ego is possible; our deductions about it are all inference. Therefore, one of the names of Prakriti is anumana.

6. Prakriti is known as *jada*, meaning 'material' or 'insentient'. In Prakriti, the possibility of creating the gross exists. Here, gross means insentient, not aware. Jada is material existence minus consciousness, where there is absence of perception and cognition. Prakriti is also called *achetana*, meaning 'unconscious' or 'unconsciousness', the consciousness is absent. Prakriti contains inherent activity or motion without awareness. The meanings of achetana and jada are similar.

7. Prakriti is also known as *maya*, because it sets limits. Maya limits or defines the area in which a form can manifest, thrive and grow. Prakriti functions through cause and effect, and each effect has a limit. A cause, in general, limits the manifestation of its effects. If a seed is the cause of a tree, the effect will be a tree; it won't be fire. If clay is the cause of a pot, the effect will not be a glass pot. So, the potent cause limits the expression of the effect, and in Samkhya, this is recognized as maya. Here, maya does not mean illusion; rather it means the force which limits, creates a boundary and defines the effect of a cause. As the full potential of Prakriti can never be totally manifest, Prakriti is called maya.

8. Prakriti is known as *shakti*, because of the continuous motion inherent within it. Motion is possible, even in insentient objects. A wheel is not aware that it exists, but the function of a wheel is to move. In the same way, shakti is motion, whether conscious or unconscious.

9. Prakriti is known as *avidya*, because it is opposite to *vidya*, or knowledge. Prakriti is the unknown or unrecognized potential. For example, the potential of a seed remains unknown until it develops into a particular kind of tree, with a certain type of leaf, flower and fruit. At night, when darkness envelops everything, the colours and shapes of objects cannot

25

be distinguished, but that does not mean that they have ceased to exist. These are examples of *avidya*, where there is no perception, recognition or knowledge of an effect, whereas recognition is vidya.

This concept of Prakriti as avidya has been defined in vedantic Samkhya, rather than in Ishvara Krishna's Samkhya. Here, Prakriti is considered to be the potent and primary cause of the entire creation. This applies not just to one world or form of creation, but to hundreds of millions of worlds and forms. Some of these forms are animate and some inanimate, some sentient due to the infusion of consciousness, and some insentient. Samkhya describes every form of creation, whether gas, liquid, bacteria or human being, as an evolute of Prakriti, because it has function, action and quality. Every manifest thing may not have all these attributes; some may have only function and quality, and others may have only quality. Creation can be one-dimensional, two-dimensional, three-dimensional, four-dimensional and beyond.

What we perceive as consciousness is totally different; it seems to move with Prakriti, but is actually an attribute of Purusha. In the absence of consciousness, Prakriti simply manifests different dimensions and forms. Prakriti is known as avidya, because there is no recognition by the being or object. Samkhya says, if fire had consciousness, it would know 'I burn', but it does not have consciousness and is not aware that it burns. If water had consciousness, it would know 'I flow', but it does not have the consciousness necessary to know its own quality. We consider bacteria as animate beings but do they consciously know their own quality? Animals are animate forms with their own modes of thinking, expression and behaviour. They know that they exist and interact with other animals or people.

So, the different stages of evolution: mineral, vegetable, animal and human, are levels of Prakriti. All levels of evolution have different degrees of self-consciousness, self-awareness and self-identity. A stone is considered to be jada or inert, but if that stone suddenly gets an injection of consciousness, it will recognize and express itself as a stone. Jada is insentience, material existence minus consciousness. Avidya is not existence minus consciousness, but existence minus recognition. Consciousness is one thing and recognition is another. You may be conscious, but suddenly you recognize something. That recognition is an added realization of something within consciousness. Recognition is vidya and the absence of that is avidya. So, avidya does not mean absence of consciousness; avidya is present even in conscious beings.

10. Prakriti is known as *swatantra*, meaning the 'independent principle'. Prakriti is independent, even though all forms of creation are dependent upon it. Prakriti is not dependent on anything to manifest itself. No secondary state is necessary for Prakriti.

11. Prakriti is known as *akarana*, which means 'uncaused'. Prakriti is the root of all causes, but has no cause in itself, nor is it the effect of any cause. Prakriti is independent of any cause, yet it is the cause of all manifest existence. If you remove Prakriti, everything is removed.

12. Prakriti is *avyayava*, partless, while all manifestations have parts. Prakriti is one, whereas objects can be many. Prakriti is infinite, while the objects are finite.

13. Prakriti is called *adrishya*, imperceptible, because of its subtle nature, which is unmanifest and cannot be perceived.

14. Prakriti is *nirvaiyaktika*, impersonal, because there is absence of *buddhi*, intelligence and will.

15. Prakriti is *shashvata*, eternal, because it is beyond time and space. Prakriti gives birth to time and space in order to create. Prakriti is permanent, being the cause of all causes, while all other causes are impermanent.

16. Prakriti is *trigunatmika*, wherein the three gunas: sattwa, rajas and tamas, exist in the state of total equilibrium. The gunas are not parts or attributes of Prakriti, but constitute Prakriti as a whole. Prakriti is made up of these three gunas in the balanced state of *samya avastha* – "*Gunanam samyavastha Prakritih*".

Prakriti is known as a substance, *dravya*. In Samkhya, the three gunas are substances. They are not attributes of a substance, but are recognized as substance itself. The gunas, which are the substance of Prakriti, go through a process of combination and permutation to become the cause of the manifestation of different causes and effects.

The gunas allow the perception or recognition of Prakriti to take place. In the absence of sattwa, rajas and tamas, Prakriti would not be recognized or understood. Therefore, the final attribute of Prakriti is trigunatmika.

4

Three Gunas

Why are there three gunas? Why not one or two, or four or five? If only one guna existed, it could not be responsible for hundreds and thousands of different manifestations. One guna can be responsible for only one kind of manifestation, just as one flower seed can give birth to only one type of flower. Two gunas will always be opposing and negating each other, like day and night, sun and shade. With three gunas the possibility of myriads of existences results, and therefore, a fourth is not necessary.

The balanced form of the three gunas is known as Prakriti The gunas constitute Prakriti and are not mere attributes. The combination of the three gunas: sattwa, rajas and tamas, leads to the concept of Prakriti as a force, as dynamism. Prakriti cannot be conceived of without the three gunas. According to Samkhya, Prakriti is a substance, or *dravya*, comprised of the three gunas, which allow realization and cognition. In every manifest object these three gunas exist in the form of experience and give rise to understanding or knowledge, and from that we infer the existence of Prakriti.

Classification of the gunas

The three gunas are subtle and imperceptible. Knowledge of the gunas can be obtained only through anumana, inference. The existence of sattwa, rajas and tamas is recognized or inferred from the presence of *prakasha*, light, *kriya*, motion,

29

and *sthiti*, stability, respectively. Sattwa gives birth to the feeling of *sukha* or pleasure, rajas to the feeling of *dukha* or pain, and tamas to the feeling of *udasina*, passivity or indifference. This classification is given in the *Samkhya Karika* as follows:

Sattvam laghu prakaashakamishtamupashthambhakam chalam cha rajah;
Guru varanakameva tamah pradeepavachchaarthato vrttih. (13)

Sattwa is light or buoyant *(laghu)* and illuminating *(prakasha)*. Rajas promotes desire and is stimulating *(upashthambhaka)* and mobile *(chala)*. Tamas is heavy or sluggish *(guru)* and obscuring or enveloping *(varanaka)*. They function for a single purpose like the components of a lamp, whose purpose is illumination.

(*Samkhya Karika,* verse 13)

Every object in existence has the quality or capability to give a feeling of pleasure, sorrow or indifference. If you look at a flower, you feel pleasure, sukha. If you look at human waste, you feel disgust, aversion or rejection, which are aspects of dukha. The gunas can be observed from different angles, physical and non-physical or psychological. The non-physical attributes are *preeti*, attraction or affection, *apreeti*, rejection, non-acceptance, and *vishada* or indifference. The following chart shows the different qualities of the gunas.

Sattwa	Rajas	Tamas
Prakasha (illumination)	*Kriya* (motion)	*Nishkriyata* (passivity)
Sukha (happiness)	*Dukha* (pain)	*Udasinata* (indifference)
Preeti (attraction)	*Apreeti* (rejection)	*Vishada* (indifference)

This classification of the gunas can be illustrated by somebody receiving the results of an exam. The pass result gives the feeling of happiness, and according to this classification, happiness or sukha would come in the sattwa state. If the exam was failed, there is dukha, and according to

30

this classification, the pain or sorrow comes in the category of rajas; there is *apreeti*, rejection, aversion. Somebody who is unconcerned about passing or failing the exam would be indifferent, and this classification falls under tamas; there would be vishada or udasinata, indifference.

In the description of tamas, a difference arises between the Samkhya view in the *Bhagavad Gita* and the Samkhya of Kapila. The first chapter of the *Bhagavad Gita* is called 'Vishada Yoga', the yoga of depression. Here vishada is related to despair, but generally in Samkhya, vishada simply means indifference, where there is neither attraction nor rejection, where things do not create an impression. Udasina implies the absence of impression but it is different to the quality of witnessing. Indifference is where the mind perceives something momentarily and then leaves it, whereas witnessing is a state of total awareness, where the mind observes the object and sees the cause and effect of it.

Minute awareness is witnessing, while indifferent perception and cognition that something exists is udasina. Simply looking at a lawn, for example, is cognition or perception; you see the grass. But if you look more closely with the attitude of a witness, then you will notice the weeds in the grass. In the state of *sthitaprajna*, *sakshi* or *drashta*, you become the witness of the totality, but there is only a superficial awareness in the state of indifference. You see something, but there is no connection of that object or experience with your intellect; there is no analysis. In Samkhya, that is the meaning of vishada or udasina, cognition without the relationship of intellect.

Therefore, the quality of indifference is classified as tamasic, while the quality of sakshi bhava or witnessing is sattwic. Sattwa is the symbol of knowledge. The sattwic state in itself is luminous and has the capacity to illuminate or reveal objects; therefore the swabhava or nature of sattwa is light. Because sattwa in itself is knowledge or wisdom, the cognition of objects, forms and experiences in the physical dimension happens due to the existence of sattwa.

31

Furthermore, the nature of sattwa is to give pleasure, happiness and joy at the mental level. So, one can say that contentment, satisfaction, euphoria, happiness and bliss are the different effects of sattwa. Along with sattwa and preeti, we have illumination, prakasha.

Rajas inspires action, dynamism and movement. Rajas itself is motion and therefore it also stimulates motion in different forms, experiences and objects. The positive nature of rajas is stimulation, activation and motivation, while the negative effect is sorrow, worry, unhappiness, dissatisfaction, grief and aversion. These are some of the effects of rajas.

Tamas represents inaction and ignorance or nescience. It contradicts knowledge and action; it is in opposition to sattwa and rajas. Sattwa is an aid to attaining knowledge, whereas tamas is a barrier to attaining knowledge. Knowledge here does not mean mere intellectual knowledge, but knowledge derived from interaction, communication, cognition, understanding and realization. Tamas is also symbolic of nishkriyata, inactivity, passivity and impotency. So, tamas is in opposition to the effects of rajas and sattwa, and because of this, we experience lethargy, inactivity and lack of motivation.

Trigunatmika

Sattwa and tamas are totally inactive by themselves. Only under the influence of rajas does the combination of gunas take place so that sattwa, rajas and tamas become an experience. There would be no manifestation of either sattwa or tamas in the absence of rajas. In every manifest object these three gunas exist or function together. Therefore, Prakriti as well as the entire manifest creation are known as trigunatmika. However, in the manifest world these three qualities never occur in equal parts; rather they go through a process of combination and permutation. In any object or experience, one guna is predominant and the remaining two are secondary.

The nature of a form or an experience is determined by the dominant guna. When sattwa is predominant, things are auspicious, when rajas is predominant, inauspicious, and when tamas is predominant, indifferent. So, the pure forms of creation are sattwic, the impure forms rajasic and the neutral forms tamasic. These three concepts are important, because they are used openly and liberally in the Theory of Manifestation. According to Samkhya, *shuddha tattwas* are the pure elements representing sattwa, *ashuddha tattwas*, the impure, mixed or changed elements, representing rajas, and the neutral tattwas represent tamas.

All three gunas are contrary to each other, but in being contrary, they aid each other. For example, you can liken the three gunas to oil, a cotton wick and a spark of fire. If you try to light the oil without the wick, it won't burn. However, once the wick soaks up the oil, a spark will ignite the lamp. Oil is liquid, fire gaseous, and the wick solid, but when the three come together, the outcome is light. This example shows how three different substances come together to create a common effect, a form of manifestation. Similarly, the coming together of the three gunas becomes the cause of an experience, and creates an effect, which is the manifest world.

Swaroopa and viroopa parinama

According to Samkhya, the gunas are continuously in motion or *parinama*. The gunas constantly intermingle, changing their form. This change of form has two aspects: swaroopa parinama and viroopa parinama. *Swaroopa parinama* means the merging of a guna in a form comprised of the same guna. For example, if sattwa converts into sattwa, rajas into rajas, and tamas into tamas, that is swaroopa parinama. *Viroopa parinama* is the merging of a guna in a form comprised of different gunas. Viroopa parinama occurs in the following three circumstances:

1. when sattwa merges into rajas or tamas
2. when rajas merges into sattwa or tamas
3. when tamas merges into sattwa or rajas.

Viroopa parinama is the type of transformation seen at the time of creation, manifestation and destruction. Swaroopa parinama only happens when Prakriti is in a state of equilibrium, then the tattwas or elements merge back into themselves in the state of samya avastha, total equilibrium, and there is no creation. Samya avastha is Prakriti's real or basic form, known as *moola*, primordial, or *avyakta*, unmanifest Prakriti.

5

Purusha

Purusha means pure consciousness, which is a separate principle from Prakriti. In Samkhya, the differences between Purusha and Prakriti are described as follows.

1. Purusha is sentient whereas Prakriti is insentient.
2. Purusha is *trigunatita*, beyond the three gunas, whereas Prakriti is *trigunatmika*, composed of the three gunas.
3. Purusha is the knower, *jnata*, whereas Prakriti is that which is known, *jneya*.
4. Purusha is inactive, *nishkriya*, whereas Prakriti is active, in constant motion.
5. Purusha is free from all causes and effects, whereas Prakriti is the primary cause.
6. Purusha is unchangeable, whereas Prakriti is changeable.
7. Purusha is *aparinama*, without consequences or results, whereas Prakriti is full of results, being the source of all manifestation.

Tasmaachcha viparyaasaat siddham saakshitvamasya purushasya;
Kaivalyam maadhyasthyam drashttatvamakartribhaavashcha.
(19)

Because pure consciousness (Purusha) is the opposite of that which consists of the three gunas, it follows that: it is the pure witness *(sakshitva)*, it is solitary *(kaivalya)*, it is neutral (separate from specific experience) *(madhyasthya)*, and it is not an agent *(akartribhava)*.

(Samkhya Karika, verse 19)

Purusha and Atma

The terms Purusha and Atma both mean 'spirit'. The *Bhagavad Gita* has stated very clearly that the Atma cannot be perceived by the senses; it is eternal, permanent and unchangeable. The same description has been used in Samkhya in relation to Purusha. So, Atma and Purusha are different names for the same concept. In the *Samkhya Karika,* the word Purusha has been used rather than Atma. When the word Purusha is used, it refers to a nature which is self-contained, although it is abstract. The Sanskrit definition of Purusha is: *Puri shete iti purushah. Shete* means that which is 'dormant' or 'inactive'. The word *puri* here means the body, which is the citadel of the senses, mind and spirit.

So, the consciousness in creation and beyond creation, that eternal nature which is based on wisdom, knowledge and self-realization, is known as Purusha. The nature of Purusha is *chaitanya*, which means self-awareness, that which is intrinsically aware, luminous and enlightened. That awareness is known as *shuddha chaitanya*, pure awareness. Purusha is beyond pleasure and pain, because it is free from *raga* and *dwesha*, attraction and repulsion. Raga and dwesha are both the result of desire, but Purusha is desireless, there is no desire aspect in Purusha. The laws of cause and effect do not bind Purusha, nor is it connected with any sinful or virtuous act.

Controversy between Samkhya and Vedanta

An interesting confrontation takes place between Samkhya and Vedanta at this point. In Advaita Vedanta, Shankaracharya assigns three attributes to Atma: *sat,* truth, *chit,* consciousness, and *ananda,* bliss. In Samkhya, ananda is associated with sattwa. Samkhya argues that Purusha is trigunatita, beyond the gunas, so bliss cannot be an attribute of Purusha, only *sat*, eternal truth that is pure, fixed and luminous, and *chit*, total consciousness which is devoid of any guna. Ananda cannot be an attribute of Purusha because no experience that stems from the manifestation of a particular guna affects Purusha. If Purusha were to experience bliss, then it would also experience the opposite of bliss, and be subject to duality.

In order to free the concept of Purusha from the nature of duality, Samkhya has to reject the vedantic theory of ananda being part of the nature of spirit. It is interesting to note that in reply, Shankaracharya gives a different definition of ananda, which accords with his Advaita Vedanta philosophy. He argues that there is a difference between sukha, happiness or bliss which relates to sattwa guna and the manifest world of the senses, and ananda, which relates to transcendental bliss beyond the gunas.

Five proofs of the existence of Purusha
In order to clarify its views, and respond to challenges from other schools, Samkhya formulates five arguments for the existence of Purusha. The five natures of Purusha are: (i) sanghat pararthatvat, (ii) trigunadi viparyayat, (iii) adhishthanat, (iv) bhoktri-bhavat and (v) kaivalya.

1. Sanghat pararthatvat
The first quality called on to establish the existence of Purusha is *sanghat pararthatvat*, which refers to objects that are created to provide some benefit to the user. For example, a bed is constructed to enable a person to sleep well. Samkhya argues that, similarly, the mind, body, senses, intellect and ego are used to provide instruction or entertainment for something else, namely Purusha. So, Purusha is the enjoyer of whatever is created in the world. Purusha is the witness. For example, a grandfather sitting in a chair, watching his grandchildren play cricket, is not participating in the game. He is simply an observer. He knows the rules of cricket and sees the children

making mistakes, but he allows them to do so. In the same way, Purusha is the *drashta*, the witness, the seer, observing the play of the senses, mind, intellect, body and ego. The play is directed by Prakriti, but the actual realization of what is happening out there in the realm of Prakriti is being recognized by Purusha, the drashta. So this argument states that the purpose of the sanghat implies Purusha.

Ishvara Krishna also says that Prakriti does not derive any enjoyment; Prakriti is only a sequence of effects. If you are running, you are not observing yourself or your environment, but the person who is watching you run sees where you are. Therefore, it is wrong to say that Prakriti has created this entire manifest, visible dimension and the unmanifest, invisible dimensions for its own cognition and gratification. Prakriti develops and evolves into different forms and different objects, visible and invisible, in order to aid Purusha in recognizing its own nature – that is the meaning of sanghat pararthatvat.

The idea is that Purusha is the seer of the play of Prakriti. Purusha realizes that Prakriti is the doer, and that whatever Prakriti does is to enable Purusha to know its own nature.

Purushasya darshanaartham kaivalyaartham tathaa pradhaanasya;
Pangvandhavadubhayorapi samyogastatkritah sargah. (21)

For revealing the entire dimension of Prakriti to Purusha, and for liberation (*kaivalyartham*) of Prakriti, there is conjunction or association (*samyoga*) between Purusha and Prakriti, like the cooperation between the lame and the blind. From this association proceeds creation or manifestation.

(*Samkhya Karika*, verse 21)

Purusha and Prakriti are associated like a lame man and a blind man, who are both separate, yet cooperate to their mutual advantage. The function of Purusha is to provide sight and the function of Prakriti is to provide motion and from this association proceeds creation or manifestation. So, Purusha witnesses the play of Prakriti, and Prakriti performs for the benefit of Purusha.

To understand this concept it should be remembered that Prakriti by itself is in samya avastha, a state of total equilibrium, where there is no manifestation, it is *avyakta*. Only in the proximity of Purusha does Prakriti become active. Take the example of a magnet, which does not manifest any force unless a piece of iron is placed close by, then the force of attraction manifests. Prakriti, being insentient, is like the iron and Purusha, being sentient, is like the magnet. Purusha is self-aware; the nature of consciousness is inherent in Purusha, like the attraction inherent in the magnet. Prakriti has all the possibilities of manifestation, but does not become active until it comes into the proximity of Purusha.

Therefore, Prakriti cannot manifest without Purusha, nor can Purusha observe in the absence of Prakriti. Purusha cannot be the drashta in the absence of Prakriti, because there would be nothing to see. Prakriti cannot express its inherent nature and qualities without Purusha to witness them; what would be the use of creation? Without the seer, the avyakta, moola prakriti subsists quiescently, and every-thing remains in balance and harmony, in samya avastha. But in the presence of the Purusha, as an automatic response, Prakriti begins to unfold and manifest, just as iron naturally gravitates towards a magnet. Although the iron and the magnet are independent, both are also interdependent, and their roles are clear.

In Advaita Vedanta, Shankaracharya has said that the nature of Atma (the pure consciousness also known as Brahman or Purusha) is threefold: truth, consciousness and bliss. Samkhya says that bliss is not a characteristic of Purusha, because bliss is a manifestation of sattwa and Purusha is beyond sattwa and all the three gunas. If we confirm that Purusha is beyond the effect of the three gunas, that it is pure consciousness, pure existence, pure awareness, pure truth, the unchangeable principle beyond time and space, then bliss cannot be an attribute of Purusha. But then, how does this concept apply if Prakriti's role is to manifest for the benefit of Purusha?

In Sanskrit, the word *bhokta* is widely translated as 'the enjoyer'. However, the literal meaning is one who 'sees', one who 'experiences' what is happening. If there is a plate of appetizing food and you just see it, that is one thing. However, if you wish to eat it, then you become involved. So, *bhokta* has two meanings: (i) one who is conscious, and (ii) one who is the performer, the actor and the enjoyer. A reaction takes place within you due to the input of an object or a subject that you either like or dislike. However, if you can avoid any involvement with, or reaction to the input, and simply observe it, even then you can be called the bhokta, but not in the same sense as when you are interacting and reacting with the object.

When you are neither involved nor interacting with the object, then you are simply an observer, or drashta. The best example is watching a movie. You may simply watch the movie as a witness. However, if you begin to laugh and cry as the actors enact their drama, then you become the involved, reactive bhokta, because you have identified with the events depicted in the movie. You are feeling what is happening on the screen, interacting with it and reacting to it, so you become part of the act. However, if you simply sit and watch without any personal participation or reaction, then you are also a bhokta, but with another form of perception and cognition.

Therefore, the assembly of all the different causes and effects in the world, which are cognized only at the time of creation or manifestation, are for the bhokta, the drashta, and the witness participation of Purusha. This argument is known as sanghat pararthatvat.

2. Trigunadi viparyayat

The word *triguna* means 'three gunas' and *viparyaya* means 'false knowledge'. So first, the definition of *triguna* should be revised. Prakriti is composed of the three gunas, which are not attributes or qualities, but together constitute Prakriti. These three constituents of Prakriti are also substances, *dravya*. On the other hand, Purusha is *atriguna*, having no substance of the three gunas. Purusha witnesses the interplay of the three gunas, but knows that this is only interplay, not the original manifestation. This is where *viparyaya*, or false knowledge, arises, because the combination of the three gunas is an altered state and does not reflect their true nature. Upon seeing the altered state of the three gunas, one may believe in the reality of that particular manifestation or state, but Purusha knows that the altered form of the three gunas is unreal or false, *mithya*.

Purusha realizes the falsity of the manifest nature and, because of this realization, does not become involved in the interplay of Prakriti. The gunas are never static. In their combinations and permutations, there is always more of one and less of the others; they never manifest in their true nature or full potency. There is always an imbalance, which gives rise to an altered effect. An unbalanced cause creates an unbalanced effect, which is not a true representation. Only when Prakriti itself is in *samya avastha*, perfect balance, is the true nature of the gunas represented. However, when the gunas start associating and creating other causes and effects, they leave their balanced nature and take form according to unbalanced causes and effects.

Therefore, Purusha recognizes every experience that arises due to cause and effect as viparyaya, false knowledge or perception. For example, in the distance you see a wisp of cloud and think it is smoke, or you see smoke and think it is a cloud. Both ideas are wrong, because you are supposing what it could be, without knowing the reality. However, Purusha knows what is illusion and what is reality. All external manifestation is viparyaya to Purusha, because it knows the reality behind the appearance. But one who does not know the reality speculates and creates further ideas and concepts, which become causes for further effects. Purusha does not do that, because it is *sarvajnata*, omniscient.

Thus, the second proof of the existence of Purusha is based on the idea that there must be something beyond the three gunas. That something is defined as Purusha, because it is Purusha's nature to recognize the false or illusory knowledge arising from the gunas, *trigunadi viparyayat*. We know that all the objects and experiences in the world are comprised of the three gunas in different intensities. All the forms and objects in creation cause *sukha*, happiness, *dukha*, unhappiness or affliction, and *udasinata*, indifference, due to the effects of the three gunas. However, there has to be some element, which is *atriguna*, 'not of the three gunas' or 'beyond the three gunas'.

3. Adhishthanat

The third concept called on to establish the existence of Purusha is *adhishthanat*, which refers to things coming from an original source. Purusha has been known and recognized as the overseer, especially in the form of inspiration. Just as a car will not move until it is started by the driver, in the same way Prakriti and all the insentient objects of Prakriti do not become active until they receive guidance or force from Purusha. The insentient objects can only become dynamic and active when there is a conscious faculty guiding, directing or inspiring them to function and act. In the same way Prakriti and its different permutations have a guide. Purusha is the guide of Prakriti and its allied effects, and can provide them with conscious force or movement.

Or, more accurately, Prakriti is not guided by Purusha, rather it is infused with its force. Just as the attraction in a magnet is inherent in the magnet and infuses the iron, so Prakriti is influenced by the inherent quality of Purusha. Just the presence of Purusha induces Prakriti to act. Purusha does not do anything; rather it acts like a catalyst in a chemical reaction. The word *adishthana* also comes from the root *stha*, meaning 'fixed in its own axis'. Things are happening around Purusha so, being fixed, it becomes the centre. Although it is not the actual performer or actor, still it automatically becomes the centre of the movement.

Tasmaattatsamyogaadachetanam chetanaavadiva lingam;
Gunakartritve'pi tathaa karteva bhavatyudaaseenah. (20)

Because of the conjunction *(samyoga)* with Purusha, the
insentient evolute *(achetana lingam)* of Prakriti appears
to have consciousness; similarly the neutral consciousness appears to have agency, though all agency is solely
due to the three constituent gunas.

(Samkhya Karika, verse 20)

4. Bhoktri-bhavat
All the manifest objects that are perceived produce feelings
of pleasure, aversion or indifference. But who is it that
recognizes these feelings which are derived from the different
manifest forms? Prakriti cannot recognize the nature of its
creation, because Prakriti itself is insentient, so the cognizer
of the feelings which emanate from the interaction with
different objects in creation is known as Purusha. Purusha
exists as the seer, not only as a passive cognizer, but as an
alert cognizer of everything that takes place in the realm of
Prakriti. The seer, or bhokta, of the various effects cannot be
Prakriti. The concept of bhokta was discussed in relation to
sanghat pararthatvat.

5. Kaivalya
The fifth quality called on to establish Purusha is *kaivalya*,
which means aloneness, freedom or liberation. This is a
dharmic concept because the effects of Prakriti, which are
composed of the three gunas and their side effects:
attraction, repulsion and indifference, are considered to
be the cause of bondage. Purusha cannot be liberated
from the clutches of Prakriti by continuously enjoying the
play of life; however, there comes a time when the
consciousness turns away from the experiences of the
world. If you watch the same film over and over again,
absorbing each and every scene, finally a time will come
when you turn away and stop watching it.

43

Also, the inherent nature of Purusha is to observe and, at the same time, remain aloof from the attraction or bondage of Prakriti. When Purusha turns away from the play of Prakriti, it is no longer the bhokta of pain and pleasure, happiness and sorrow, or indifference. That state in which there is no input of the effects of Prakriti on Purusha is known as kaivalya. When Purusha stops watching the effects of Prakriti, what he observes is kaivalya, aloneness, which is also called *moksha*, liberation or freedom. The concepts of moksha and samadhi presuppose the existence of Purusha.

As an analogy, I am the observer, sitting quietly, while people are writing notes and thinking, "Oh, this is a very complicated subject," or "This is very simple," or "This is very interesting". Thoughts are going on in people's minds and creating different expressions on their faces, while I am simply observing. When I get tired of watching them, I close my eyes and then I do not see the multiplicity; that is Purusha.

Drishtaa mayetyupekshaka eko drishtaahamityuparamatyanyaa;
Sati samyoge'pi tayoh prayojanam naasti sargasya. (66)

The one witness, Purusha, thinks, "I have seen her". The other, Prakriti, thinks, "I have been seen" and ceases her activity. Though the association between them (*samyoga*) persists, there is no motive for further evolution.

(*Samkhya Karika*, verse 66)

Purusha is the source from which Prakriti derives the inspiration to become active. Purusha observes the play of Prakriti, and also looks away from Prakriti in order to experience aloneness, oneness or completeness. The concept of oneness is the concept of Purusha. While Purusha observes Prakriti, it sees the duality or multiplicity, and there is no identity of oneness, or kaivalya. However, when Purusha turns away from the multiplicity and duality of Prakriti, it becomes aware of the oneness, of kaivalya. That aloofness or loss of contact between Purusha and Prakriti makes Prakriti return

44

to its balanced state. The entire manifestation of Prakriti is withdrawn when Purusha stops cognizing it. So, in kaivalya, Purusha identifies with its own nature, not with the nature of Prakriti, while Prakriti also reverts back to its original state. The natural outcome of conscious, external involvement is gradual withdrawal after some time. After opening the eyes, there is recognition, then closing the eyes and centering within oneself. This is the daily rhythm of life; after extroversion in waking awareness comes the period of withdrawal into deep sleep awareness. The in-built faculty for withdrawal is closing the eyes. After visual stimulation, we want to rest our eyes and we close them. This natural response in life is similar to the response at the level of Purusha. For ages, Purusha has been watching the play of Prakriti and then it closes its eyes.

The understanding from which this theory evolved is expressed in Vedanta as the day and night of Brahman. During the day of Brahman, the world existence comes into being, and during the night everything is withdrawn into Brahman. This is dissolution, or *laya*, merging back into the Self, where everything dissolves back into its original source. In Advaita Vedanta, Brahman is the single source; in dualistic Samkhya, Purusha is separate and Prakriti is separate. Prakriti depends upon Purusha's consciousness in order to become active. When Purusha cuts the external consciousness, then Prakriti becomes inactive and returns to samya avastha, the unmanifest state.

Theory of Causation
When Purusha and Prakriti come together, manifestation takes place. Prakriti needs Purusha to provide a direction for its activities. Purusha is like a person who cannot walk, and Prakriti is like a person who cannot see. In order to complete the process of manifestation, Purusha rides on the shoulders of Prakriti. In this way, the conscious faculty of Purusha guides the movement of Prakriti. The only role of Purusha is to guide and the only role of Prakriti is

to manifest. Prakriti cannot see or cognize, but it has the faculty of movement, whereas Purusha cannot move, but it has consciousness.

The insentient Prakriti manifests only when Purusha shows the direction. Purusha also says to Prakriti, "That is enough riding on your shoulders for me, now it is time to be still." The moment Purusha gets down from Prakriti's shoulders, the conscious faculty of knowing, observing and analyzing ceases. Prakriti then falls back into its original state of *jada*, insentience. In this way, Purusha and Prakriti are two separate principles, which enable each other to fulfil their roles in evolution. Only when Purusha and Prakriti come together and the impulse is given to move, does mahat or buddhi come into existence. This buddhi is not the intellect that we have in our mind, but the supreme intelligence responsible for the subtle, causal movements and manifestations of all the evolutes of Prakriti, which have the potency to become active and dynamic and to create.

We have discussed Karyakaranavada and Satyakaryavada and the Theory of Causation, which involves Purusha and Prakriti. The next subject is *Siddhantavada*, the Theory of Manifestation.

6

Theory of Manifestation

According to the Samkhya system, there are twenty-five stages in evolution, which are classified into three categories as follows:
1. Consciousness, beyond the manifest and unmanifest
2. Unmanifest
3. Manifest.
Purusha, representing the totality of consciousness beyond the manifest and unmanifest, is number one. Prakriti, alone with itself, the unmanifest, avyakta or moola prakriti, where all the three gunas are in harmony and balance in samya avastha, is number two. The third category relates to the manifest state, *vyakta avastha*, where the twenty-three components or expressions of Prakriti are seen.

The role of mahat
The manifest evolution begins with mahat, the first evolute of Prakriti. The meaning of *mahat* is 'great'. Amongst all the evolutes of Prakriti, mahat has the most prominent and subtle existence. Mahat is the subtle and prominent cause for the manifestation of the other twenty-two *tattwas*, or elements. The experience of the entire universe is contained in mahat as though in a seed, and from a broad perspective, mahat represents the aspect of universal presence. The attributes of Prakriti are present in it universally. Mahat is also considered to be *hiranyagarbha*, the womb of Prakriti, in which the

combinations and permutations of the different elements take place to bring forth manifestation.

Another word for mahat is *buddhi*, which is translated as the supreme intelligence. Samkhya uses the word buddhi to mean mahat and the two words are interchangeable, although in other philosophical systems this is not always the case. In Samkhya, this supreme intelligence has two functions: decision and ascertainment, *nirnaya* and *avadharana*. In the aspect of intelligence, buddhi has the ability to differentiate between the knower, knowledge and what is to be known. The meaning of buddhi that we are more familiar with is in relation to day-to-day discrimination. For example, if I have an experience of pleasure or pain, that experience is physically an inherent expression of myself caused by an 'x'factor. Through the manifest buddhi, which is my intellect, I can differentiate between:

1. My status as a person
2. The experience, that is creating an awareness of
3. An 'x' factor and its expressions, which I recognize as pleasant or painful, positive or negative.

Therefore, even in normal mundane life, the word buddhi is used for discrimination and knowledge.

Adhyavasaayo buddhidharmo jnaanam viraaga aishvaryam;
Saattvikametadroopam taamasamasmaadviparyyastam. (23)

Buddhi (intellect, intuition) is characterized by will and reflective discerning *(adhavasaya)*. Its sattwic nature has four forms *(roopa)*: appropriate behaviour *(dharma)*, discriminative knowledge *(jnana)*, non-attachment *(vairagya)* and auspicious attainments and perfection *(aishwarya)*. Its tamasic forms are opposite to these in nature.

(*Samkhya Karika,* verse 23)

Buddhi manifests in the form of sattwa and tamas. The nature of sattwa is illumination, light, and the absence of limiting or restricting conditions. The result of luminosity,

48

when combined with knowledge and discernment, gives rise to four different effects, which are dharma, jnana, vairagya and aishwarya. *Dharma* means virtuous nature; *jnana*, differentiation between real and unreal, true and false; *vairagya*, non-attachment; and *aishwarya*, auspicious attainments, mastery and perfection. The opposite nature consisting of the limiting and binding factors is seen in tamasic buddhi. This is where a clear distinction is made in the roles of Prakriti. Tamasic buddhi confines a person to the world and sattwic buddhi liberates a person from the world.

Reflection theory
At a higher level, the activity of mahat in the form of supreme intelligence is necessary to distinguish the difference between cause and effect. Mahat creates awareness in Purusha of the activities that are guided by Prakriti, and aids Purusha to maintain its distinction from Prakriti. The pure conscious factor of Purusha is reflected in mahat. Prakriti itself is insentient, but through mahat, the first evolute of Prakriti, the sentient aspect of Purusha is reflected into creation. So, mahat is known as supreme intelligence or buddhi, but in the sense of pure intelligence, the higher form of buddhi, not just intellect.

You see the reflection of a flower in a mirror; the reflection can be seen, but it is not the actual flower. Similarly, the consciousness of Purusha is mirrored in mahat, but the conscious factor in mahat is not Purusha, it is just a reflection. Mahat is not self-luminous as it is one of the evolutes of Prakriti. So, the proximity of Purusha to Prakriti infuses Prakriti with a reflection of consciousness which is used to start a process of activity. In the process of manifestation, it is not used to know itself, but for the process of externalizing and activating the potentials of Prakriti. However, it can also be used to discriminate and analyze the potentials of Prakriti.

The conscious factor of Purusha becomes the catalyst to create the first evolute of Prakriti, mahat, where the combinations and permutations of the gunas take place.

49

Mahat, therefore, is trigunatmika, within the realm of the three gunas. Mahat is influenced by the first change in the balanced state of the gunas. All three gunas exist in mahat. When sattwa is predominant the qualities which manifest are: knowledge, wisdom, virtue, non-attachment and excellence. When tamas predominates, the qualities of mahat are: ignorance, vice, imperfection, attachment and impotence, which are the opposite of the sattwic qualities. Rajas vitalizes the process.

As mahat is a conditioned reflection of Purusha, there is always a contradiction between the changeless Purusha and mahat, which is continuously changing under the influence of the three gunas. In this way, the conscious factor of Purusha is reflected in mahat, and the role of the consciousness is diluted. In daily life, the components of buddhi, ahamkara and manas are all influenced by the gunas. The combinations of sattwic, rajasic and tamasic ahamkara become grosser and more down to earth. This is the process of manifestation or evolution according to Samkhya. So we shall look into the diluted form of the potentials, which are inherent in all these different layers and structures. The next evolute is *ahamkara* or ego.

Ahamkara and its evolutes

Mahat or buddhi is ultimately responsible for the emergence of ahamkara, the cosmic ego, and for existence in the form of a unit, which means not as a whole, but in fractions. Each fraction is identified as an independent unit, whether it is in the form of senses and sensory perceptions, the elements or the subtle substance of the elements. Each fraction is identified by its nature and quality, and that identification and recognition of the different components is the function of ahamkara. The individual 'I' is always the finite self; it can never be the infinite Self. The 'I' does not exist in the infinite Self.

Ahamkara is the recognition of, and identification with, the conditioned potentials in Prakriti, because Prakriti contains karana, cause, within itself. Those causes are the conditioned potentials, but in their unmanifest form they are

50

universal; they are not confined to an identity or a form as yet, but they contain within themselves the potential to manifest. The recognition of the universal, conditioned potentials is the original ahamkara. It is recognizing the inherent effects in a cause, like the existence of a tree in a seed, warmth and brightness in the sun or coolness in the moon.

25 Evolutes in Manifestation

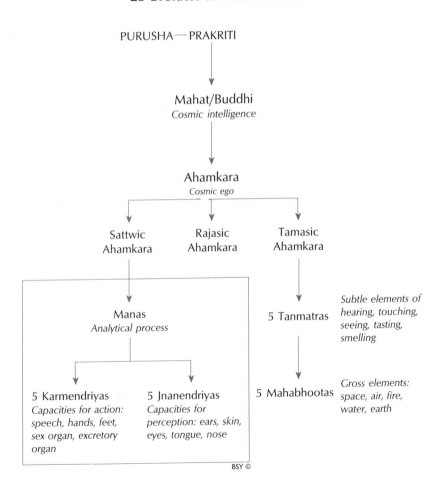

Ahamkara is the effect of buddhi, because in buddhi knowledge of the existence of an object and the perceiver is created. The first self-awareness develops in buddhi and as a result, the sense of identity, ahamkara, the ego principle, arises. Ahamkara is also influenced by the three gunas. When ahamkara is sattwic, it gives rise to knowledge of the self, 'I'. From sattwic ahamkara are born manas, the mind, the five jnanendriyas, also known as *buddhi-indriyas*, and the five karmendriyas.

Abhimaano'hankaarah tasmaad dvividhah pravartate sargah;
Ekaadashakashcha ganah tanmaatrapanchakashchaiva. (24)

Ahamkara, or egoism, is characterized by self-assertion *(abhimana)* and gives rise to a two-fold evolution, namely the group of eleven (manas, five jnanendriya and five karmendriya), and the five-fold primary or subtle elements *(tanmatra)*.

(*Samkhya Karika*, verse 24)

When ahamkara becomes tamasic, the five *tanmatras*, or subtle elements, and the associated *mahabhootas*, or gross elements, come forth. Rajasic ahamkara vitalizes the sattwic and tamasic emanations and, as a result, they become dynamic and begin to interact with each other. The rajasic ahamkara is the catalyst to complete the process of manifestation. So, there are Purusha, Prakriti and the twenty-three manifest elements of evolution: mahat, ahamkara, manas, the five jnanendriyas, the five karmendriyas, the five tanmatras, and the five mahabhootas.

Saattvika ekaadashakah pravartate vaikritaadahamkaaraat;
Bhootaadestanmaatrah sa taamasastaijasaadubhayam. (25)

The group of eleven, which is sattwic in nature, emerges out of sattwic ahamkara *(vaikrita)*. The five tanmatras emerge from tamasic ahamkara *(bhootadi)*. Both groups manifest due to the influence of rajas on ahamkara *(taijasadubhayam)*.

(*Samkhya Karika*, verse 25)

Evolutes of sattwic ahamkara

Manas comes into being from sattwic ahamkara, it is the first transformation of the cosmic activity, which has been happening at subtle and causal levels, into a manifest form of Prakriti. *Manas* should not be translated as mind; rather it is the process of thinking and analysis, *manan*. When you analyze a thought or an experience, the process is known as manan, reflection. From the first evolute of sattwic ahamkara also come the five *jnanendriyas* (*jnana-indriyas* or *buddhi-indriyas*), the organs of sensory perception, and the five *karmendriyas* (*karma-indriyas*), the organs of action.

The five jnanendriyas, are *chakshu*, the sense of sight or vision; *shravana*, the sense of hearing; *ghrana*, the sense of smell; *rasa*, the sense of taste, and *sparsha*, the sense of touch. With the jnanendriyas you derive understanding of form through seeing, hearing, smelling, tasting and touching. The eyes, ears, nose, tongue and skin are not the jnanendriyas, but the organs in which the faculties or powers of the jnanendriyas exist.

Buddhi-indryaani chakshuh shrotraghraanarasanatvagaakhyaani;
Vaakpaanipaadapaayoopasthah karmendriyaanyaahuh. (26)

Buddhi-indriya or *jnanendriya* (the sense capabilities) are: seeing (*chakshu*), hearing (*shrotra*), smelling (*ghrana*), tasting (*rasa*), and touching (*tvak*). *Karmendriya* (the capabilities for action) are: speaking (*vak*), grasping or handling (*pani*), walking or locomotion (*pada*), excretion or expelling of waste (*payu*), and sexual procreation or interaction (*upastha*).

(*Samkhya Karika*, verse 26)

The word karmendriya denotes organs which perform specific functions. The five karmendriyas are: *vak*, vocal chords; *pani*, hands; *pada*, feet; *payu*, excretory organs, and *upastha*, reproductive organs. However, it is the force inherent in the physical organs, and not the organs themselves that is meant by karmendriya. The process of speech is the actual karmendriya, not the vocal chords. The ability to grasp is the actual karmendriya, not the hands. The ability to move is the actual potency inherent in the feet. The ability to eliminate waste matter or to reproduce is the actual indriya, not the excretory or reproductive organs.

These functions are not limited to the body only, but also represent mental processes. The function of the hands is to hold, but holding is also a subtle process which takes place in the mind. Similarly, the feet relate to physical and mental movement. The excretory organs are responsible for the elimination of toxic matter, not only from the body but also from the mind. When toxic matter accumulates in the body, it is expelled through the excretory organ, but the accumulated waste must be removed from the mind as well. The reproductive organs are responsible for joy and procreation, physically and mentally.

So, the functions of the indriyas relate to the total life, not just to the physical body. They also relate to the five tanmatras and the five mahabhootas. Actually, there are eleven indriyas: five jnanendriyas, five karmendriyas and manas. In Samkhya, manas is seen as the eleventh indriya because it is the controller and receiver of the experiences gained through the other indriyas. It also directs the jnanendriyas and karmendriyas to perform their respective functions.

Ubhayaatmakamatra manah, sankalpakamindriyan cha saadharmyaat;
Gunaparinaumavisheshaannaanaatvam baahyabhedaashcha. (27)

Manas possesses the nature of both (the sensory and motor capabilities). It is the deliberating principle *(sankalpaka)* and also a sense organ since it possesses properties common to the sense organs. The multifariousness *(nanatvam)* and the external diversities (of things apprehended by the mind) arise due to the specific transformations of the gunas *(guna parinama visheshat).*

(*Samkhya Karika,* verse 27)

54

The mind has the ability to combine the different components of the sensory perceptions and to recognize them. In the absence of the mind, if you touch a rock, you won't know it is a rock. The conscious factor that links all the different impressions received through the senses is manas. By harmonizing, controlling and guiding the indriyas or senses, you are able to control the mind. Here the concepts of *indriya sanyam*, managing the senses, and *manas sanyam*, managing the mind, arise. Then you are able to disassociate yourself from sense objects, the evolutes of tamasic ahamkara, and move on the path of *mukti*, liberation.

Evolutes of tamasic ahamkara

The five *tanmatras*, or subtle elements, and the five *mahabhootas*, gross elements, are the evolutes of tamasic ahamkara. All the insentient aspects of creation, like minerals, gases, etc., are evolutes of the tamasic ahamkara as a result of the combination and permutation of these elements. In the insentient creation there is an absence of manas, karmendriyas and jnanendriyas. In sentient creation, manas and the senses exist. The human body, for example, functions because of the mind, jnanendriyas and karmendriyas. Mammals, birds and other animals have some degree of mind and senses. But for the most part this entire creation in the form of the galaxies, planets, stars, etc., is a product of tamasic ahamkara.

The quality of tamas is stability, fixed nature or gross matter. Earth has a static form, water has a form which can be recognized, fire has a form that does not change, and if the form changes, it is no longer fire. In the same way, air and space or ether have forms. Earth, water, fire, air and ether are the *pancha mahabhootas*, the five gross elements. The total manifest creation is due to the coming together of these different elements in different quantities, degrees and combinations.

These five elements are derived from the five tanmatras, which are their subtle essence. For example, when you hold a pen in your hand, you feel the gross form, but there is also the feeling of smoothness or coolness; when you hold sandpaper or a rock, you feel the rough texture, which gives you an idea about the composition of the object. Tanmatra is the subtle aspect or the essence of the element, and each element gives a different awareness in relation to its composition. However, a tanmatra is not dependent on perception. Even if you are blind and cannot see the element, it still exists and its subtle essence exists. So the tanmatras are not the sense organs; they are the natural qualities inherent in any element.

The tanmatras along with the mahabhootas give rise to physical manifestation. The senses of perception, along with the mind, give knowledge or awareness of those physical manifestations. Rajasic ahamkara is the medium through which transition takes place from the state of luminosity to the dark state of ignorance, and vice versa. Rajasic ahamkara is the force that activates or stimulates the inherent qualities in the sattwic and tamasic evolutes of ahamkara. In the absence of rajas, the inherent qualities of sattwa and tamas will never be activated or manifested. If you go along one path, from point A to B, you can also return along the same path from point B to A. The path is always two-way; transition happens both ways. Rajas is the force that allows you to shift from one stage to the next.

Process of recognition

By coming together, Purusha and Prakriti give birth to mahat, which is also known as buddhi. This is the cosmic buddhi that knows what is true and false, what is right and wrong. The cosmic buddhi differentiates between the eternity of Purusha and the impermanence of Prakriti. What is seen as manifestation is transitory and time bound. In order to transcend Prakriti, identification with the eternal has to take place, and that happens through buddhi. From buddhi comes ahamkara, the sense of I-ness. From sattwic ahamkara we have manas, the five karmendriyas for interaction and the

56

five jnanendriyas, by which the different images and impressions that we receive are recognized.

The eyes are not conscious, but the form that is seen through the eyes goes into the area of manas for reflection, analysis and observation. In manas, association and identification takes place, so manas is the conscious factor of the karmendriyas and jnanendriyas. From tamasic ahamkara we have the five tanmatras and five mahabhootas. There is no aspect of consciousness in tamasic ahamkara, only in sattwic ahamkara. In the middle, there is rajasic ahamkara, which allows you to experience either the quality of sattwa or the quality of tamas in whatever you do. But most of this activity goes on at a subtle level.

Ete pradeepakalpaah parasparavilakshanaa gunavisheshaah;
Kritsnam   purushasyaartham   prakaashya   buddhau
prayachchhati. (36)

These (the group of thirteen: buddhi, ahamkara, manas and the ten sense and action capabilities) have their own characteristic differences due to the differing modifications of the attributes *(gunavishesha)*. They function together, like the components of a lamp, illuminating all the field of experience and presenting it to the supreme intelligence (buddhi) for the purposes of Purusha (namely, experience and subsequent liberation).

(*Samkhya Karika*, verse 36)

The impressions or images that are received in the manifest physical form by the jnanendriyas, along with the actions which take place through the karmendriyas, are recognized by the faculty of manas. The eyes see a form, but they do not have the consciousness to recognize and identify the form. Recognition of an experience happening through the indriyas is the function of manas, the reflective, thinking process. Manas reflects, analyzes, compares and identifies.

57

When we speak of mind control, what is it that is being controlled? Can we control the senses, the perceptions of sound or smell? No, the indriyas, or sense organs, never stop functioning, whether in a state of sleep or wakefulness, but these processes are deeply linked with the conscious faculty of reflection. Therefore, rather than using the expression mind control, it is better to speak of analysis, comparison, reflection; putting together the picture that is received from the karmendriyas and jnanendriyas. The function of manas is only to put together the different pieces of the jigsaw puzzle and to identify it.

Manifestation of the elements

Tamasic ahamkara is responsible for the manifestation of the elements, which are divided into two categories: subtle and gross. The subtle elements are known as tanmatras, and the gross elements as mahabhootas. The tanmatras are: sound, touch, form, taste and smell. They are the subtle essence or quality of the five gross elements: ether, air, fire, water and earth. From the tanmatra of sound comes the mahabhoota of space. From the tanmatras of sound and touch, the mahabhoota of air emerges. From the tanmatras of sound, touch and form, the mahabhoota of fire emerges. From the tanmatras of sound, touch, form and taste, the mahabhoota of water emerges. Then from all the five tanmatras: sound, touch, form, taste and smell, comes the mahabhoota of earth or matter.

So, one of the main theories of Samkhya is that the combination of different tanmatras is responsible for the emergence of the mahabhootas. At the same time, each element has a unique quality that represents that element. For example, in earth, we find smell, because smell is the only new tanmatra in earth's composition. The special quality of water is taste, the special quality in fire is form, in air is touch and in space is sound. Even scientifically, sound always takes place through space, which is not empty, not a vacuum. Space contains the potentiality of all the other tattwas, which already exist in minute quantities. Touch is always connected with movement and movement is a quality of air. You may say that sound is also conveyed through air, but air also has the distinct quality of touch. You can relate form and fire in the same way.

The tanmatras and the tattwas are also linked with the karmendriyas and jnanendriyas. The sense organ linked with earth is the nose; with water, the tongue; with fire, the eyes; with air, the skin; with space, the ears. This is how the subtle elements, the five tanmatras, manifest in the form of the five mahabhootas, and connect with the five jnanendriyas to make a complete realm of experiencing the manifest nature of Prakriti.

The twenty-five elements enumerated in the *Samkhya Karika*, from Purusha to the mahabhootas, include thirteen organs of recognition, action and assimilation. They are classified in two categories: internal organs and external organs. Manas, ahamkara and buddhi are the three internal organs through which you can work in the realm of understanding and knowledge. In this realm there is the inherent possibility of knowing the past, present and future. These three internal organs are known as the *antahkarana*. The *bahirkarana*, or external organs, are the five karmendriyas and the five jnanendriyas. So in the bahirkarana there are ten organs, and in the antahkarana there are three organs, which makes thirteen organs.

Karanam trayodashavidham tadaaharanadhaarana-
prakaashakaram;
Kaaryam cha tasya dashadhaa'haaryam dhaaryam
prakaashyam cha. (32)

The thirteen-fold instrument (mahat, ahamkara, manas, five karmendriyas and five jnanendriyas) is the basis of seizing *(aharana)*, holding or sustaining *(dharana)* and illuminating *(prakasha)*. The objects that are seized, held and illuminated are of ten kinds.

Antahkaranam trividham dashadhaa baahyam trayasya vishayaakhyam;
Saampratakaalam baahyam trikaalamaabhyantaram karanam. (33)

The internal instrument *(antahkarana)* is threefold, and the external *(bahya* or *bahirkarana)* is tenfold providing the sense contents *(vishaya)* of experience. The external instruments function in the present and the internal instruments function in all three times *(trikala)*.

(*Samkhya Karika,* verses 32-33)

The five tanmatras are the subtle essences used to identify or connect the antahkarana with the bahirkarana. The tanmatras are the essences that form a relationship between the mahabhootas, which make up the universe of manifest nature, and the cognition of those forms of creation that happens through the karmendriyas, jnanendriyas and manas. So the tanmatras and mahabhootas are not counted in either the antahkarana or the bahirkarana. Purusha and Prakriti are also not included in either the antahkarana or bahirkarana. Purusha is not included because it is pure knowledge. Prakriti is not included because it is the primary material cause. So twelve elements are not included in the differentiation between antahkarana and bahirkarana.

Saantahkaranaa buddhih sarvam vishayamavagaahate yasmaat;
Tasmaat trividham karanam dvaari dvaaraani sheshaani. (35)

Because the supreme intelligence (mahat or buddhi) together with the other internal instruments comprehends the entire field of objects, the three-fold internal instrument can be called the door-keeper *(dvarin)* and the tenfold external ones are the doors *(dvara)*.

Ete pradeepakalpaah parasparavilakshanaa gunavisheshaah;
Kritsnam purushasyaartham prakaashya buddhau prayachchhati. (36)

60

These (the group of thirteen: buddhi, ahamkara, manas and the ten sense and action capabilities) have their own characteristic differences due to the differing modifications of the attributes *(gunavishesha)*. They function together, like the components of a lamp, illuminating all the field of experience and presenting it to the supreme intelligence (buddhi) for the purposes of Purusha (namely, experience and subsequent liberation).

(Samkhya Karika, verses 35–36)

At the time of reversal or dissolution, *laya,* all the five mahabhootas, five tanmatras the five karmendriyas, five jnanendriyas and manas merge back into ahamkara. Then ahamkara merges back into mahat and mahat merges back into Prakriti. Kaivalya or 'separation' of Purusha from Prakriti then takes place, which leads us into the concepts of bondage and liberation.

7

Bondage and Liberation

There are three forms of suffering, due to which an idea arises in Purusha that it is bound. Whenever the three gunas are active, there is disharmony, and dealing with disharmony causes struggle. This conflict and suffering has been divided into the three categories of: *adhibhautika*, *adhyatmika* and *adhidaivika*. The first kind of pain stems from material causes, the second from personal, inner causes, and the third from cosmic or divine influences.

When Purusha, being the conscious nature, identifies with the three classifications of suffering, it appears bound. Prakriti is the cause of all sufferings, but does not identify with them, because Prakriti does not have consciousness. We interact with the pains and pleasures of the world according to inherited or innate predispositions, *bhavas*, and end up either further entangled in karma or detached from it.

Dharmena gamanamoordhvam gamanamadhastaad-bhavatyadharmena;
Jnaanena chaapavargo viparyayaadishyate bandhah. (44)

Through the predisposition towards virtuous nature (*dharma*) one ascends to higher planes of existence; through inappropriate or vicious behaviour (*adharma*) one descends to lower planes. Through knowledge

comes release and by its reverse (i.e. *avidya* or ignorance) one becomes bound.

(Samkhya Karika, verse 44)

When Purusha is freed from the influences of mahat (buddhi),
ahamkara and manas, it is *chetana*, pure consciousness. However,
when Purusha comes into contact with Prakriti, it forgets its
own nature. Due to this ignorance, Purusha identifies with
intellect, ego and mind, and begins to believe it is not different
from the experiences it has in the realm of Prakriti. This
association of Purusha with Prakriti causes bondage through
false identification. It is like reacting to a dream. While dreaming
that somebody is chasing you with a gun, you experience fear
and anxiety. But upon awakening, you realize it was just a
dream. The nature of Purusha is totally conscious, which can be
related to the state of wakefulness. However, when Purusha
interacts with Prakriti, the consciousness becomes dissipated.

While sitting alone in a room you become introspective,
absorbed in your thoughts and nature, but when somebody
walks in, you come out of that state. You look at the other
person and start communicating, forgetting about yourself.
The same thing happens with Purusha. While Purusha is
independent, it is perfectly at peace with itself. But when
Prakriti comes before Purusha, it begins to interact with
Prakriti. At that time, the awareness is dissipated. Interaction
and then identification begins due to association with Prakriti.
Purusha loses its self-consciousness and begins to observe
and react to the nature of Prakriti. Because of this loss of
awareness and self-identification, Purusha thinks, "I am the
bhokta, the enjoyer" and begins to identify personally with
the experiences of buddhi, manas and ahamkara, which are
manifestations of Prakriti.

*Sookshmaah maataapitrijaah saha prabhutaih tridhaa
visheshaah syuh;*
Sookshmaasteshaam niyataa maataapitrijaa nivartante. (39)

63

The subtle *(sukshma)* body, and the body born of mother and father *(matapitrija)*, together with the objects made of the gross elements *(prabhoota)*, are specific. Of these, the subtle body is constant, and continues to exist from one life to the next, whereas the gross body born of parents perishes.

(Samkhya Karika, verse 39)

Tatra jaraamaranakritam duhkham praapnoti chetanah purushah;
Lingasyaavinivrittestasmaadduhkham svabhaavena. (55)

Therein Purusha experiences suffering brought about by old age and death on account of non-cessation of the subtle body (linga). Therefore pain is the very nature of things.

(Samkhya Karika, verse 55)

At this point, Purusha becomes a witness to the experience of pain, pleasure and indifference, due to identification with the effects of Prakriti and its trigunatmika nature. The natural and inherent consciousness of Purusha recedes further from awareness as Purusha identifies with the dance of Prakriti. That identity gives rise to the feeling of bondage, "I am limited, I am confined, I am only seeing, knowing, understanding and experiencing what is being shown to me by Prakriti." Due to the influence of the three gunas Purusha experiences bondage, and the ability to discriminate is lost. Now, the question arises as to why Purusha, being conscious, is affected by the role that Prakriti plays. This can be answered in the following way.

Parents become happy when their children do something positive and constructive, and unhappy when they do something destructive or negative. Although the parents are different to their offspring, they respond to the activities of their children because of an emotional relationship or connection. Similarly, a relationship exists between Purusha and Prakriti, and therefore Purusha is not able to separate its own role from the role of Prakriti and begins to think, "I am not different to the intelligence which guides Prakriti." In this way, Purusha becomes totally identified with buddhi and forgets that buddhi (mahat) is the product of Prakriti. This wrong identification or lack of discrimination is the cause of bondage. It is similar to parents identifying with the suffering of their child. Although the parents are not suffering, still they sit beside the child's bed, knowing they cannot do anything to alleviate the suffering.

Means of liberation

According to Samkhya, knowledge or *jnana* is the medium of liberation. Knowledge here means to know the difference between being and non-being. In Samkhya, final liberation is not attainable through karma, because liberation attained through karma would only be of an impermanent nature. So, Samkhya says that jnana, wisdom, is the medium of *mukti*, liberation. At night, while walking on the road, you may see a rope and mistake it for a snake, but by shining a light on it, you realize it is not a snake, but a rope. Similarly, through the light of wisdom you can distinguish between being and non-being. This wisdom is known as *samyaka jnana*, ultimate knowledge, which means balanced, integrated awareness of Purusha and Prakriti.

This knowledge is not a product of the mind, because the mind is an evolute of Prakriti. In Samkhya's theory of evolution, manas is an evolute of the sattwic ahamkara, and whatever knowledge you have through manas will always be within the limits of sattwic ahamkara. It won't even take you as far as mahat. How do you transcend ahamkara and mahat in order to have that final knowledge, where you can differentiate between reality and unreality? Samkhya says that ultimate knowledge cannot be obtained through the mind and senses; it can only be attained through control and mastery of the senses and the mind. In order to accomplish this mastery, Patanjali's *Yoga Sutras*, which is based on Samkhya, has propagated the eight-fold path of *ashtanga yoga*: yama, niyama, asana, pranayama, pratyahara, dharana, dhyana and samadhi.

Manan is contemplation; *nididhyasana* is repeated meditation. Samkhya maintains that repeated contemplation and practice are necessary in order to attain the highest knowledge, to know the difference between being and non-being, and to re-establish Purusha in its own true identity or *swabhava*. This can be attained through ashtanga yoga, which provides the path for contemplation and practice. In this way, ashtanga yoga becomes a method for the liberation of Purusha. In the state of liberation new gunas do not emerge or become active; rather samya avastha, the balanced state of the gunas, is attained. Then Prakriti ceases to manifest and Purusha becomes self-aware. Just as we wake up from a dream, heave a sigh of relief, and say, "Thank God that was only a dream," in the same way, at the time of liberation Purusha becomes self-aware and realizes, "Oh, I am free. I was under the hypnosis of Prakriti. In that state of hypnosis I was identifying with the evolutes of Prakriti, but now I realize that I am free."

The state of liberation means the destruction of ignorance, desire and vice, as well as the removal of virtue, because virtue is sattwic. Liberation is a state of total cessation of activity in the realm of the gunas. Samkhya does not consider liberation to be blissful or even enjoyable, but just the absence of suffering. In other traditions, like Vedanta, liberation is said to be *satchidananda*, truth-consciousness-bliss, but Samkhya says it is the total cessation of all activity. Once all activity ceases, there is no bliss, because *ananda* is an evolute of sattwa, and the state of liberation is *trigunatita*, a state beyond the three gunas.

Process of liberation
Samkhya describes the concept of *mukti* or *moksha*, liberation from the cycle of birth and death, and mentions two related states. The first is jivanmukti. As soon as the self realizes the

difference between Purusha and Prakriti, and merges into its own nature, it becomes free, but in *jivanmukti*, the body continues to live, because the past karmas are not destroyed at this stage. The karmas accumulated from the past have to be gradually discharged, so the body remains. Like a potter's wheel it takes time for the rotation or cycles of life to gradually slow down and stop. The momentum accumulated in the past by the rotating wheel of karma carries on, although the Purusha is separate or free.

Samyagjnaanaadhigamaaddharmaadeenaamakaaranapraaptau; Tishthati samskaaravashaachchakrabhramivaddhritashareerah. (67)

Through the attainment of perfect, discriminating knowledge *(samyagjnana)*, dharma and the rest (the seven predispositions) become devoid of their causal efficacy. Yet, one continues to be invested with the body *(dhrita sharira)* due to the force of latent dispositions *(samskara)*, just like a potter's wheel continues to rotate due to the momentum transferred to it by the potter.

(Samkhya Karika, verse 67)

So, although the consciousness is free in a jivanmukta, the body and other attributes carry on with the momentum of the past karmas until those karmas are totally dissolved. Further births may be necessary to complete that karma. Samkhya believes that even after being liberated, one may be reborn to fulfil past karmas, but still have a liberated mind. For example, there is the story of Jada Bharata, a great king, who did sadhana and attained moksha. Afterwards, he took several births in order to exhaust the residual karmas. In each birth his mind was totally detached from the body but still the subtle body had to go through its own processes until the karmas accumulated by its past bodies were finished.

The second concept is of *videhamukti*, where the accumulated karmas are totally annihilated. In this case, the body dies and the liberated soul remains in the bodiless state. In the absence of karma there is no further rebirth for the videhamukta, unless one so chooses.

Tasmaanna badhyate'sau na muchyate naapi samsarati kashchit;
Samsarati badhyate muchyate cha naanaashrayaa prakritih.
(62)

Therefore, Purusha is never really bound, nor is it ever liberated, nor does it transmigrate. It is only Prakriti who in her various manifestations, is bound, liberated and transmigrates.

(*Samkhya Karika,* verse 62)

Although Purusha is never really affected by the attributes of Prakriti, it still identifies with the transformations which Prakriti brings about. For example, you do not see your own face until you look in the mirror. At that time you say, "So, that is what I look like," and you form an image of yourself. Afterwards, even if you don't look into the mirror again, you retain that impression of yourself. Similarly, Purusha is never involved with the manifest forms, but due to association with Prakriti, it is caught in the wheel of life and death because of identification. Even now, if your consciousness was liberated due to contemplation and meditation, and you were to enter samadhi, still the body would have to fulfil its span of life.

The body contains those images and impressions, which hold it together. This has been described in the *Bhagavad Gita* as *deha buddhi.* The personal experience of evolved beings is that the body still pulls them back. The same images carry on and life continues until those impressions are totally cleared. In this life you may suddenly realize, "Oh, that is not me!" Then you may start erasing, but you cannot wipe the entire blackboard clean in one sweep, because the blackboard is always bigger than the duster. Although you may be free and have the right attitude, still you can only

68

eradicate one samskara or karma at a time. It takes another sweep to remove another samskara or karma, and one life is necessary for each sweep of the board. In jivanmukti, you return and bring with you your original clear state. There is no involvement. You are simply wiping out the past; you are not creating new karmas. There is no involvement with Prakriti to create new karmas.

Subtle and gross bodies

Samkhya believes in two bodies, *sukshma sharira*, the subtle body, and *sthoola sharira*, the gross body. The gross body is composed of the mahabhootas, whereas the subtle body is composed of the tanmatras, jnanendriyas and karmendriyas, manas, ahamkara and mahat. What we are seeing here is a three-tier concept. The sthoola sharira is the body that takes birth and dies. The sukshma sharira is the body that transfers from life to life until all the karmas are exhausted. Purusha is the pure consciousness at the level of the realized soul.

Sookshmaah maataapitrijaah saha prabhutaih tridhaa visheshaah syuh;
Sookshmaasteshaam niyataa maataapitrijaa nivartante. (39)

The subtle *(sukshma)* body, and the body born of mother and father *(matapitrija)*, together with the objects made of the gross elements *(prabhoota)*, are specific. Of these, the subtle body is constant, and continues to exist from one life to the next, whereas the gross body born of parents perishes.

Poorvotpannamasaktam niyatam mahadaadi sookshma-paryantam;
Samsarati nirupabhogam bhaavairadhivaasitam lingam. (40)

The mergent or subtle vehicle *(linga)* pre-exists all other bodies *(purvotpanna)*, is unattached or unconfined *(asakta)*, is constant or persistent *(niyata)*, and is composed of tattwas beginning with *mahat* and ending

69

with *tanmatras* (intellect, ego, mind, ten capabilities and the five subtle elements). It is free or devoid of experience, transmigrates or reincarnates and is tinted or scented by the basic predispositions *(bhava).*

(Samkhya Karika, verses 39–40)

Consciousness, body and mind are not all one unit. The *Bhagavad Gita* has also said that whenever the soul has to go into the realm of Prakriti, it does so via the sukshma sharira. The sukshma sharira does not die when the gross body dies, but continues until it exhausts its karma. After the karmas are exhausted, it merges with consciousness, Purusha. Only then is videhamukti, complete freedom from the cycle of birth and death, attained. The sequence of rebirth stops there.

8

Plurality of Purusha

Relating the concept of Purusha to human consciousness led Samkhya to the theory of Purusha's plurality. There are five arguments for the plurality of Purusha, which are given as follows:

1. Birth and death: Samkhya says that if Purusha were one, everybody would take birth and die at the same time. This would also mean that creation stops after the death of the body, because if Purusha withdraws after the death of the body, then Prakriti becomes redundant. However, that is not what happens in the natural world. Prakriti is never seen to be redundant; rather, there is continuous transformation, birth and death. To explain the concept of Purusha from a physical, material point of view, it is assumed that a new aspect of Purusha comes into being with each birth, and with each death that aspect of Purusha dissolves back into its source. This implies there is not only one, but a plurality of Purushas.

2. In each individual there are different degrees of manifestation in the jnanendriyas and karmendriyas. This point is linked with the fourth and fifth points.

3. There are differences in nature and personality. If Purusha were one, then no matter how many people there are, they would all be clones, identical to each other. It would be like planting only roses in a garden; no matter what their colour may be, they would all represent a particular

uniform nature. In the world we do not see this type of uniformity. Some people are theists, some atheists; some are dynamically involved in society, others have withdrawn from social involvement. The mentality and nature of individuals differ, which indicates the involvement of Purusha with Prakriti at different levels, not at one level.

4. In the theory of evolution, there is movement from mahat, or buddhi, through sattwic, rajasic and tamasic ahamkara, to the tanmatras, karmendriyas, etc. The primary nature is mahat and the secondary nature is ahamkara with its three divisions; these are the two main natures. Each person identifies differently, and according to his or her understanding sees the world either from a perspective of knowledge or of ego, whether it is tamasic, rajasic or sattwic ego. Since there is no uniformity in perception and evolution, the Purusha cannot be the same in everyone.

5. At each stage in life different gunas, which are independent realities, become predominant. Sometimes sattwa is predominant, sometimes rajas or tamas. Due to the environment and the combination of other causes and effects, a particular guna becomes predominant. For example, if one goes into depression, tamas becomes predominant, and that quality will affect the functions of the karmendriyas and jnanendriyas. If one becomes aggressive, rajas will become dominant, and that quality will affect the functions of the karmendriyas and jnanendriyas. A dictator may be a highly knowledgeable person, who knows how to manipulate and influence people's minds and natures, but his nature is one of domination. If the guna is rajasic, the function of the jnanendriyas and karmendriyas will be to dominate. If a person becomes sattwic, that will also affect the functions of the karmendriyas and jnanendriyas. We can see this illustrated in the Buddha, who is the image of tranquility, peace and indifference to the world. The expression of the jnanendriyas and karmendriyas was different in him.

This relates to the second point. For each person, at each stage, the environment and even the karmas alter the quality of the gunas; they can make you sattwic, rajasic or tamasic. Therefore, Purusha cannot be one because each person responds differently to the same situation.

Process of identification

The actual vision of Samkhya is that on one side you have Purusha and on the other side you have Prakriti. When they are separated, Purusha is self-contained and Prakriti is in samya avastha or balanced integration. When they come into contact with each other, for whatever reason, Prakriti begins to evolve as mahat or buddhi, the higher intellect; ahamkara, which is the sattwic, rajasic or tamasic self-identity, and then manas and the indriyas, which we use in life in order to function, express and transcend.

Throughout this process, if Purusha is watching Prakriti, it is observing mahat, the sattwic, rajasic and tamasic ahamkara and all the lower manifestations. Purusha is omniscient only when it is disassociated from Prakriti. For example, I may be alone in the room, thinking, reflecting and analyzing. In this process of contemplation, reflection and analysis, I observe the totality that comes into the field of my perception. But the moment I interact with somebody, I block out the thoughts, experiences and feelings which I was aware of previously, and relate to that one person only. In this way, Purusha's state of omniscience becomes limited or focused while interacting with Prakriti.

First, Purusha becomes aware of mahat as a separate unit. Next, Purusha becomes aware of ahamkara as separate from mahat. While Purusha is focused on mahat, it is not focusing elsewhere. At night, if you shine a torch, the light will illuminate only one object at a time. In order to observe many objects at a time, you need a light which encompasses your entire field of vision. So, when Purusha is moving from the state of *sarvajnata,* omniscience, to a stage of *ekadhyana,* awareness of one thing only, it is like shining a torch on one object only. Similarly, when sitting as an observer in the audience, watching a dance performance, you are not able to

73

watch all the performers at the same time. You can only observe one at a time clearly and distinctly. Through peripheral vision you may see the other dancers and their movements, but only when you focus on one do you actually observe the *bhava*, the mood, the *mudra*, the attitude or gesture, and all the other details. In the same way, when Purusha identifies with buddhi, it observes or focuses only on buddhi. The three gunas make up Prakriti, and sattwa, rajas and tamas interact with buddhi and ahamkara. Depending on which guna is predominant in buddhi, a person will experience only that influence.

For example, Shri Rama suffered from depression after returning from his guru's school, the *gurukul*. The sages of that time had recognized Rama as an *avatara*, a representation of cosmic consciousness. How could an avatara with cosmic consciousness go into a state of depression? We do not understand why this happens, so we say, "Oh, he had to play the role of a human being". Surely an avatara may play the role of a human being due to some kind of influence or situation, but he has the wisdom and knowledge to realize what the compulsion and situation is. Shri Rama is known as *Purushottama*, the highest consciousness, but in the realm of nature one goes into depression, becomes dynamic, or goes into ecstasy due to the intensity of the force in the guna. At this level of human nature, sarvajnata, omniscience, is no more; you have to identify with one aspect of buddhi or ahamkara, whether it is sattwic, tamasic or rajasic. In this way, once within the realm of manifestation, Purusha identifies with the most active principle, while ignoring the other factors.

Karmic momentum

If this process of identification were the only factor, the whole creation would stop after the span of one lifetime, as soon as jivanmukti is attained. But karma is the other factor that arises within each being, and karma impedes the attainment of jivanmukti. A potter's wheel continues to move with its own momentum and only stops gradually. In samya

74

avastha, the balanced state, there is no momentum, but from mahat onwards there is continuous momentum. The more Purusha is involved with mahat (buddhi) and the ego, the more the momentum increases, like adding fuel to the fire. So, the momentum that has become part of mahat, ahamkara, manas, personality, karmendriyas and jnanendriyas, does not stop after death, even in jivanmukti.

Therefore, Samkhya states that everyone has two bodies. The sthoola sharira, or gross body, is composed of the mahabhootas. The sukshma sharira, or subtle body, is composed of mahat, ahamkara, manas, karmendriyas, jnanendriyas and tanmatras. Whatever is created, due to the mixing of the three gunas and Prakriti's evolutes, is recognized as the body, which takes birth and dies. So, birth and death relate to the gross and subtle bodies only and that has nothing to do with Purusha. The gross body takes birth and dies. The subtle body is the other dimension in which the impressions gathered from each life's interactions are stored at the unconscious level. If these impressions were conscious, one would know the difference between what is limiting and what is liberating. The impressions come to the conscious level in the next life and become the seed of the samskaras and karmas, which are known as *pratyaya*.

Cause of re-birth

Pratyaya is a concept also used in the *Yoga Sutras* as well. Even in ananda and asmita samadhi, which are the final stages of samadhi, one has to get rid of the last pratyayas of ahamkara in order to become established in mahat or buddhi. Yoga says that the final samadhi is ananda, the samadhi of bliss. Samkhya says bliss relates to sattwa and, therefore, liberation is beyond that. Yoga agrees that only the stage up to mahat can be reached through the practice of introspection and contemplation. Bliss is experienced in mahat due to the existence of the three gunas. Final liberation is attained only when mahat is transcended and one becomes a videhamukta. So there is still the possibility of coming and

75

going, experiencing transmigration, for a person who has attained ananda samadhi.

This explains why birth and death relates to the gross body, which is below the level of ahamkara and mahat and has nothing to do with the ultimate experience of Purusha. The gross body is only the vehicle. You trade in a car when it is old, but not the driver. The important body is the sukshma sharira, which transmigrates from vehicle to vehicle, but both bodies are interrelated. People are born at different levels because the impressions that are gathered in one lifetime are carried forward into the next birth by the sukshma sharira, and that is all part of the cosmic dance. When the gross body takes birth, it becomes the vehicle for the expression of the pratyayas which were gathered in the subtle body. The highest reference in the subtle body is mahat or buddhi; below that is ahamkara, and below ahamkara are the pratyayas, which are impressions and archetypes. The impressions can be equated with samskaras and archetypes with karmas, the terms are used interchangeably, but the actual concept is this, and all these are contained within the realm of Prakriti.

The aim of Purusha is to attain moksha, or freedom from the clutches of Prakriti. Therefore the subtle body needs a gross body in order to release its karmas and this is why the subtle body enters into a gross body, causing another birth, then another and another. Moksha is attained by transcending the pratyayas, ahamkara and mahat, everything which composes the subtle body; that is the concept of liberation. Videhamukti means one has transcended both gross and subtle bodies. Jivanmukti means that one is held in, or pulled back into, the gross body in order to disentangle pratyayas. Purusha is beyond it all. However, for us, further identification on the level of the gross body creates more bondage.

The method prescribed to clear the pratyayas, ahamkara and mahat and to realize the purity of Purusha is contemplation, *manan*, and repeated meditation, *nidhidhyasana*. Contemplation and meditation are the means to liberation. In the *Yoga Sutras* there is a reference to *brahmi vritti*, another

76

subtle vritti which is beyond the five vrittis of *pramana, viparyaya, vikalpa, nidra* and *smriti*, and which leads to transcendence. A boat is necessary if you want to cross a river. Similarly, in order to transcend, there has to be a basis. The boat that takes you from one side of the river to the other is brahmi vritti, which must be awakened and developed in order to attain liberation.

Transformation of consciousness

Returning to the concept of the plurality of Purusha, human beings are not the only life form in creation. Mineral life, vegetable life, animal life, human life, divine life and transcendental life are the major categories into which creation has been classified. So, Purusha must be plural, because all the other life forms are also evolutes of Prakriti and, therefore, contain an aspect or reflection of Purusha.

Everything that exists contains spirit or consciousness; even a stone has some degree of consciousness. Consciousness has different expressions. The consciousness makes decisions when you are active and confront a situation, but in the dream state the decisive faculty of consciousness is not there. In the deep sleep state, even the visual aspect of consciousness is not there. Similarly, there is an involvement of Purusha at each level of manifestation. If Purusha were not involved, those beings would not be created. So, Purusha is many, because there is spirit or consciousness in every form that exists, animate or inanimate.

Ityeshah prakritikrito mahadaadivisheshabhootaparyantah;
Pratipurushavimokshaartham svaartha iva paraartha aarambhah. (56)

Thus, this evolution caused by Prakriti, from mahat down to the gross elements *(bhootas)*, operates for the sake of the final release of each separate self. It appears as if Prakriti were acting in her own interest, but in reality she acts in the interest of others.

77

Vatsavivriddhinimittam ksheerasya yathaa pravrittirajnasya;
Purushavimokshanimittam tathaa pravrittih pradhaanasya. (57)

Just as the secretion of milk, which is unintelligent, happens for the growth and nourishment of the calf, the action of the root cause (Pradhana) is for the sake of liberation of consciousness (Purusha).

Autsukyanivrityartham yathaa kriyaasu pravartate lokah;
Purushasya vimokshaartham pravartate tadvadavyaktam. (58)

Even as people engage in activity to relieve desires, so also the unmanifest Prakriti *(Avyakta)* functions for the sake of emancipation of Purusha.

(Samkhya Karika, verses 56–58)

According to Samkhya, Prakriti is responsible for creation; Purusha is sentient, but is not responsible for creation. Through consciousness each being has the potential to transform and change. Prakriti becomes active because of close proximity to Purusha. Therefore, Purusha is involved at each and every level of Prakriti's creation and dynamism, not as an active participant, but as a passive observer, which sees, inspires and guides. Purusha is involved as a witness. Prakriti is insentient, so there has to be somebody to appreciate it. A flower can't tell itself it is beautiful. Somebody has to acknowledge the flower's beauty. Purusha is that which appreciates and acknowledges the states of Prakriti, although it is not a participant in the creative activity of Prakriti. Purusha says, "I acknowledge this state and I support you!" So, there is appreciation.

In *Stalking the Wild Pendulum,* the scientist, Isaac Bentov mentions a very interesting concept. Describing the role of consciousness or the observer in quantum physics, he states that the process of observing changes the thing observed. The consciousness that exists in a rock or a mineral is dormant or inactive, like the state of deep sleep in a human being. In deep sleep, there is no awareness of anything, but consciousness remains. Even if the rock is made into a *murti*, an image or idol, the consciousness within it will remain dormant as long as it is left alone. But the moment you identify the murti as something and project your feelings, faith and devotion onto it, the consciousness changes. Stimulation causes an awakening to take place in the nascent consciousness of the rock, and it enters the dreaming stage.

In dream, the consciousness is not aware, but at the same time it is active. If the piece of rock continues to be the object of adoration and reverence, and you give your consciousness to it in this way, its dream state will eventually become illuminated. A stone like the *shivalingam*, the symbol of consciousness, in Baidyanath Dham, Deoghar, towards which people have expressed their faith and devotion for many generations, has become vibrant, illuminated. Whether this shivalingam is seen as Shiva, as a rock or as a hole in the ground covered with water is not important. The reality is that generations of people have awakened the consciousness of that stone with their faith. So, it has consciousness, it is vibrating, it is illuminated

Similarly, there are other crystalline forms. Crystal recharges itself and holds the personal energy directed towards it. Crystal is a rock that becomes very active when in contact with subtle energy fields.

9

God in Samkhya

Finally the question arises as to whether the Samkhya system is atheistic or accepts the existence of God. How can God be understood? Not as a human being, but as cosmic consciousness. God can't be known by the senses or the mind, which are conditioned. Initially you have to work through the conditionings of consciousness in order to become free. How can the transcendental reality be understood with a non-transcendental mind? The misconceptions about God arise because man imagines God in his own image, but God is not a physical person.

The spirit inherent in everyone is an extension of God. Just as space is all pervading, God is all pervading. The moment a form or shape is created, the infinite becomes finite, contained and identifiable, similarly, the individual spirit is contained within the body. In the *Bhagavad Gita*, Sri Krishna says that the individual consciousness is an extension of the cosmic consciousness. The individual consciousness is bound by the senses, mind and ego, but the cosmic consciousness is free from the senses, mind and ego. The individual consciousness is subject to the karmas of the body and the environment in which one lives. The cosmic consciousness is not bound by any object, space or time. So God means the non-changing principle, something that is eternal, continuous and constant, and the reflection of that nature exists in everyone as Purusha.

According to Samkhya, the seat of the transcendental nature is Purusha, which is the highest dimension in life. The supreme consciousness has come down from that high place to this low place. We have come down from there to here, and we have to use the same stairs to climb back up. These stairs represent the evolution through the twenty-five elements described in Samkhya. Therefore, Samkhya is not an atheistic system, because it acknowledges the omniscient nature of Purusha. In Samkhya, God is not known as Brahma, Vishnu or Shiva, but as the highest Purusha. Samkhya recognizes that all beings, when they reach the level of omniscience, become the supreme Purusha. Ultimately, my nature is not limited or confined; it is omniscient.

However, most people find it difficult to relate to or differentiate between the various levels of consciousness. They cannot comprehend the concept of an omniscient Purusha, because consciousness has not been studied in depth. Whatever people know about consciousness is superficial, and the mind gets caught up in the logical problems of plurality. Why does Samkhya say there is a plurality of Purushas? If you think rationally, the many Purushas are the little I's, and the cosmic Purusha is the supreme consciousness. That supreme nature is called God, but Samkhya has not given any specific name to the highest Purusha, whereas other traditions have created symbols for God, such as Brahma, Vishnu and Shiva. So, Samkhya is not atheistic, but it is the only theistic system that has not given a name to the highest Purusha.

Ultimately, Purusha is one. If a man becomes a father, his progeny will not be himself, but will be linked to him genetically. Just as the father is one, Purusha is one, and there are little ones, which arise from him. If you study Ishvara Krishna's *Samkhya Karika*, you will find that it is theistic. The philosophy of Samkhya was propounded in very early times, when God was considered to be all-pervading and did not need a special symbol for identification. Later, different beliefs, traditions and sects arose, each with its own interpretations and symbols of God. Then these different groups said to Samkhya, "Where is your symbol?"

Yoga also has no symbol, no reference to any God with form, but should it be considered atheistic or theistic? Yet Samkhya was criticized for accepting a formless God. The sects that arose after Samkhya said that Samkhya should acknowledge a form of God if it is theistic. They believed that God must be *sakara*, with form, and that any philosophy that conceives of God as *nirakara*, without form, or any philosophy that avoids referring directly to a form, is atheistic. But the real difference here is not between theistic and atheistic; it does not refer to the belief in God, but to the form or formlessness of God. Yoga is also a nirakara philosophy. In pure yoga there is no particular form of God. I may worship Shiva, you may worship Lord Jesus, and someone else may worship Allah, and that is a personal affair. For those who feel God must be sakara, with form, yoga does not have an image, so they would classify it as atheistic. But for those who accept omnipresence and omniscience as the inherent nature of God, both yoga and Samkhya would be considered theistic, although their concept of God is nirakara, formless.

Some scholars say that Samkhya does not believe in the existence of God, but it accepts the authority of the Vedas. The Vedas represent knowledge, and knowledge is manifold. Any knowledge without the concept of a higher knowledge is never complete; knowledge is a continuous and endless process. If you believe in logic and wisdom, then you are a believer; you do not have to bow your head in front of an image to become a believer. Ice is the sakara form of water. You can give ice any shape, but once the ice dissolves the nirakara remains.

Sectarian discussions enter the domain of philosophy at different points in history, but such problematic discussions should be avoided, because they are endless. If you know the basic concepts and try to analyze and understand them in your own mind, you will find that Samkhya affirms the nirakara stage of realization.

Praapte shareerabhede charitaarthatvaatpradhaanavinivritteh;
Aikaantikamaatyantikamubhayam kaivalyamaapnoti. (68)

When separation from the gross body *(sharirabhede)* has taken place and Prakriti, as the root cause (Pradhana), ceases to operate, having accomplished the purpose of Purusha, Purusha attains liberation *(kaivalya)* that is both complete or absolute *(aikantika)* and final or permanent *(atyantika)*.

Purushaarthajnaanamidam guhyam paramarshinaa
samaakhyaatam;
Sthityutpattipralayaashchintyante yatra bhootaanaam. (69)

This profound secret *(guhya)* knowledge for attaining the aim of Purusha has been expounded by the great sage *(rishi)*. In it, he has considered the duration *(sthiti)*, origin *(utpatti)* and ultimate dissolution *(pralaya)* of beings.

(*Samkhya Karika,* verses 68–69)

10

Samkhya and Yoga

Both Samkhya and yoga aim at reversing the process of awareness which at present is identified with the senses and the external objects. That awareness has to be disassociated from the objects and redirected internally to experience our spiritual nature. That experience of Purusha, the pure consciousness, may be termed as samadhi, moksha, nirvana, self-realization or union with the higher self. However, the problem is that we identify with the sensory objects that give us pleasure. We condition ourselves to think that we are not able to live without these objects, and this is the beginning of attachment, *asakti*. The association of the mind and senses with an external object creates attachment. Attachment is a strong magnetic force which holds the mind down to the experience of the pleasure that we are searching for though our senses. The time comes when we suddenly find that all of the attachments in life serve no purpose, because one day we have to leave them.

In yoga, that experience is known as *abhinivesha*, the fear of disconnection. The moment we realize that we are going to be disconnected from our kith and kin, society and family, body and mind, and that we, as we know ourselves to be, will cease to exist, fear arises. Abhinivesha is mentioned in Patanjali's *Yoga Sutras* and is often translated as the fear of death, but it is more than that; it is the fear of disconnection.

The fear of disconnection arises because we are tamasic by nature. Tamas has to be understood in the right perspective. Tamas is not a bad or negative thing; it is a conditioned state of existence. For example, a lump of clay can be shaped into a pot. Once it takes that form it is identified as a pot and not a lump of clay. The experience of identifying ourselves with our conditioned nature, and the inability to extricate the awareness from that limited nature is known as tamas. The quality of tamas expresses itself throughout life in the form of different psychological, social and religious conditionings. Tamas creates the belief patterns which we have to struggle to change, overcome or transcend as we develop.

Tamas itself is not negative, but negativity is an expression of this conditioning when change is rejected. Aggressive reaction to change is identified as a negative outcome of the tamasic conditioning. The principles of Samkhya and yoga aim at understanding how we are conditioned. Because we are in tamas as long we are in this body, and cannot live without tamas, we need to understand the components of life and existence which interact with each other and take us through the various conditionings. Samkhya and yoga give us an understanding of this process, and help to free us from the impressions created by our conditioning. The impressions created by the conditioning of tamas, rajas and sattwa are known as samskaras. Or, to put it another way, *samskaras* are an expression of the conditioned state of tamas, rajas and sattwa.

Understanding of Samkhya

We have to work through the samskaras in pratyahara and dharana meditation before experiencing the higher levels of consciousness. In this process, yoga is the practical aspect and Samkhya is the theoretical aspect. Yoga is influenced by Samkhya. Sage Patanjali, who codified the system of raja yoga, is also considered to be an exponent of the Samkhya tradition. In the past, there were eighteen schools of Samkhya.

Just as yoga is popular today, Samkhya was once a popular system because it gave an understanding of how we become conditioned and how we can free ourselves from that conditioning.

Samkhya gives us an understanding of how the senses work, how the mental states interact with the senses, and of the nature, interplay and attributes of the gunas at an individual and cosmic level. It gives an understanding of the relationship between the mind, ego and higher intellect. Samkhya gives an understanding of the manifest, *vyakta,* and the unmanifest, *avyakta,* dimensions, and how as human beings our consciousness and mind interact in these various dimensions.

Some time ago, the scientists discovered that the entire universe is comprised of only 5% white matter and the remaining 95% is black matter. So, from the scientific point of view, the universe is created of white matter and black matter. This is what yoga and Samkhya have been talking about, but in different terminology. The black matter that they talk about in science is the moola prakriti, the primordial energy, the primordial source, in which everything is fused, like a seed. The seed has the possibility of developing into a tree, but if you look at the seed, you cannot see the leaves, the wood, the flowers and fruits, although the potential exists.

The potential inherent in the seed is actualized when the conditions are right. In order to actualize the potential of the seed, you have to plant it at the right time. If you provide water, compost and protection, the potential of the seed will be seen as a small sprout, which will eventually grow into a big tree. But the inherent potential of the seed will not manifest unless the conditions are right. In the same way, the moola prakriti, or the dark matter, contains Prakriti, the potential of creation and individual identity, as well as Purusha, the unified awareness or God. Everything is within it. The 5% of white matter is the ever-expanding manifest universe, the created aspect that we experience through our instruments, body, senses, mind and ego.

This understanding is important, because it creates awareness of another dimension of existence beyond the body. The material body is only one expression of the total life; the insects, reptiles, birds and mammals all have bodies. All these different life forms are expressions of that cosmic force known as moola prakriti, the primal energy, interacting in this world and taking different forms. When the form is dissolved, the association with the objective world is severed. Then the consciousness becomes free to experience another dimension of life, to express itself in another dimension of existence, and this is known as evolution.

Clearing the ground
In yoga, evolution is explained as the movement of consciousness from chakra to chakra. There are twenty-one chakras which are important in life. At the human level there are seven, from mooladhara to sahasrara. Prior to the human level, there are seven chakras, and beyond the human level, there are seven more. These twenty-one chakras indicate the development and transformation of human consciousness, and the overcoming of various conditionings which restrict the awareness and perception of other realities. At present, our perception and performance are limited and restricted. We often do the wrong thing, despite knowing what is right.

Prior to the great war chronicled in the *Mahabharata*, when Shri Krishna was speaking with the two parties, Duryodhana, the head of the Kauravas, said, "I know what is appropriate, right and just, but I have no attraction towards that. I understand what is inappropriate, negative and detrimental, but I am attracted to that. I don't know what is making me act in this unrighteous manner. Despite knowing what is right, I want to do the wrong thing. I cannot extract myself from this state." What Duryodhana said 5,500 years ago still holds true in our life, even today.

Shri Krishna later explained to Arjuna in the *Bhagavad Gita* that we are unable to extract ourselves from our conditioning, because we identify with the drive and the search for pleasure, which clouds our wisdom. The senses, mind, emotions and ego, all have their own gravitational pull. Depending on what aspect is strong, we gravitate from one to another without any clear sense of identity or awareness of what each force is. When confronting an adversary, we identify with aggression, anger, hatred and jealousy. When meeting a friend, we identify with the feeling of friendship, affection, love, and we desire to be in close proximity to that friend. When gravitating towards money, we identify with greed and possessiveness. So each association gives birth to a different conditioned state of mind.

The different systems of yoga provide techniques to sensitize our awareness and to sublimate the passions which drive us, so we can understand what is influencing us from gross to subtle levels, and so that these conditionings can be recognized and rooted out. If gardeners want to convert a weed patch into a beautiful flower garden, first they must clear and prepare the ground to ensure that no undergrowth will restrict the growth of the new seeds. Similarly, in yoga, the ground of our head and heart must be cleared of arrogance, avarice, greed, frustration, anger, depression, anxiety, fear and insecurity before a transformation of consciousness can be experienced. Trying to practise meditation with all of this mental conditioning is like throwing seeds on top of unprepared ground and hoping that the seeds will come up. First the ground must be cleared if you want to connect with your spirit, which is the ultimate aim of yoga.

Therefore, yoga does not begin with meditation. You must clear the ground first, otherwise yoga will never flower in life. Clear your mind and heart of aggression, frustration, tension, anxiety, adversity, insecurity, phobia, hatred, jealousy, competitiveness and ego reactions; yoga will flower only when the ground is clear. The yoga practices clear the mind and heart of the associations and attachments which obstruct both growth of consciousness and liberation of energy. Awakening to our true nature is the aim of Samkhya and yoga. Samkhya gives the theoretical basis; yoga provides the tools for dissociation of the mind from the external senses, which opens our eyes internally and leads the awareness away from the search for pleasure, towards inner harmony, balance and awakening.

Development of spirituality
Two things have influenced the quest for eternal life: disease and death. If there were no disease or death, there would be no yoga, no Samkhya, and no philosophy of life. Disease and death have prompted generations of humanity to find a solution. Various systems of therapy have developed to overcome disease, and different spiritual philosophies have evolved to overcome death. Samkhya is the original philosophy of humanity, prior to any religion. Samkhya was the first philosophy to explain the connection between the individual, the universe and the controller of life and death, Purusha or God. The Samkhya tradition and philosophy has a direct relevance to yoga, as many of the yogic principles have been influenced by Samkhya.

There is a story about a blind person and a lame person who are travelling together. The blind person cannot see but has the use of his legs, and the lame person cannot walk but has the use of his eyes. So the lame person, sitting on the shoulders of the blind person, directs the way. The blind person follows his instructions, and together they reach the desired destination. The blind person is Prakriti, nature with the ability to act, perform and create, but not to analyse, understand or know. The lame person is Purusha, the consciousness which can see, think and plan, but has no ability to move. So everything happens to please Purusha, the consciousness, because only Purusha can see what is happening. Prakriti creates, but Purusha observes. All created beings are the product of this play between consciousness and energy.

Consider what was the state of the universe before the Big Bang, and what happened after the Big Bang. The

89

gases, clouds and radiations intermingled with each other, giving birth to the different elements, the tattwas, as it has been described in the Samkhya tradition. From nothingness we came into this existence and our appearance has been nothing short of a miracle. We are the product of a miracle and the miracle does not end here. The sequence of miracles continues in our life, whereby we again realize the source of our existence. The discovery of the source is the spiritual journey. This is how the idea of spirituality developed and this is the definition of spirituality: connection with the source.

Journey back to the source

The source is not influenced by the notion of time, space and object, or by our ideas and impositions of thoughts. The source is known as Self or God. This concept of God or divinity is not the religious concept; rather it indicates the transcendental nature which is responsible for working this miracle of creating something out of nothing. The tree grows from a seed. The inherent potential in the seed develops into something much greater and more beautiful than it originally was. We have also grown from the seed of our parents. At conception our journey of life begins, in which all the instruments, the senses, mind and intelligence, the positive and the negative aspects of life, come into play. The ideas of just and unjust, right and wrong develop, and we realize our nature, limitations, qualities and strengths. The Samkhya system enumerates the elements that we have to become aware of in our journey back to the source.

There are different approaches to achieve the source. Samkhya is the scale or ruler, with the millimeter notches, and it can encompass the whole universe, manifest and unmanifest. The scale of Samkhya has twenty-five notches. One notch is Purusha, the second Prakriti, the third mahat, the fourth ahamkara, and like this the system evolves. Samkhya enumerates the elements as they have evolved from nothingness into existence. It gives knowledge of creation, life and the subtle principles which influence our behaviour

90

patterns. The way to experience Samkhya is through yoga. The way to move through the twenty-five tattwas in the scale of Samkhya is by the path of yoga. Samkhya is the map; yoga is the vehicle. You can navigate your car by observing the map of Samkhya. While you are driving, you have to become one with the car. A driver has to feel the car, the power of the engine, and the movement of the clutch. He or she must know when to put the indicators on, when to use the handbrakes. A driver can't just sit in the car like a passenger. If the driver is unaware, an accident is bound to happen. But if you are in tune with the car, then you will know beforehand about anything that may go wrong; you will just feel it intuitively and make adjustments. Similarly, while practising yoga, you have to follow the map of Samkhya, attune yourself to the principles of yoga and keep going towards what is real.

Appendix

Samkhya Karika

Samkhya Karika of Ishvara Krishna

Sanskrit Text, Transliteration and Translation

दुःखत्रयाभिघातात् जिज्ञासा तदपघातके हेतौ ।
दृष्टे साऽपार्था चेत् नैकान्तात्यन्ततोऽभावात् ॥ 1 ॥

Duhkhatrayaabhighaataat jijnaasaa tadapaghaatake hetau;
Drishte saa'paarthaa chet naikaantaatyantato'bhaavaat. (1)

When one is afflicted by the three kinds of suffering *(dukhatraya)*: internal *(adhyatmika)*, external or due to nature *(adhibhautika)*, divine or celestial *(adhidaivika)*, there arises a desire to know the means of terminating them. If it be said this enquiry is superfluous since ordinary remedies exist (medicines, etc.), it is not so, because these means are neither permanent *(atyanta)* nor complete *(ekanta)*.

दृष्टवदानुश्रविकः स ह्याविशुद्धिक्षयातिशययुक्तः ।
तद्विपरीतः श्रेयान् व्यक्ताव्यक्तज्ञविज्ञानात् ॥ 2 ॥

Drishthavadaanushravikah sa hy avishuddhikshayaatishayayuktah;
Tadvipareetah shreyaan vyaktaavyaktajnavijnaanaat. (2)

Means prescribed by scriptures (e.g. the performance of sacred rituals, etc.) are like ordinary remedies since they only provide means which are subject to impurity, decay and gradations. A superior method is the discriminative knowledge of the manifest *(vyakta)*, the unmanifest *(avyakta)* and the absolute knower *(jna)*.

मूलप्रकृतिरविकृतिर्महदाद्याः प्रकृतिविकृतयः सप्त ।
षोडशकस्तु विकारो न प्रकृतिर्न विकृतिः पुरुषः ॥ ३ ॥

Moolaprakritiravikritirmahadaadyaah prakritivikritayah sapta;
Shodhashakastu vikaaro na prakritirna vikritih purushah. (3)

The root cause or primordial nature or matter *(moola prakriti)*
is non-evolute (not evolved from anything else) or un-
generated *(avikriti)* and subsists by and in itself. The group of
seven beginning with the great principle or supreme
intelligence *(mahat* or *buddhi)*, ego *(ahamkara)* and the five
subtle elements *(tanmatra)* all evolve from something else,
i.e. are generated principles *(vikriti tattwa)* as well as generative
(prakriti tattwa). The group of sixteen, namely discursive mind
(manas), the five sense capacities *(jnanendriya* or *buddhi-indriya)*,
the five action capacities *(karmendriya)* and the five gross
elements *(mahabhoota* or *bhoota)* are only generated principles.
Consciousness or Self *(Purusha)* alone is neither a generative
nor a generated principle.

दृष्टमनुमानमाप्तवचनं च सर्वप्रमाणसिद्धत्वात् ।
त्रिविधं प्रमाणमिष्टं प्रमेयसिद्धिः प्रमाणाद्धि ॥ ४ ॥

Drishtamanumaanamaaptavachanam cha sarvapramaanasiddhatvaat;
Trividham pramaanamishtham prameyasiddhih pramaanaaddhi. (4)

Direct experience or perception *(drishta)*, inference *(anumana)*
and statements of reliable and competent persons *(apta-
vachana)* are the means to right knowledge *(pramana)*. All
other means of right cognition are established thereby.
Anything that can be known *(prameya)* must be established by
means of one of these reliable means of knowing.

प्रतिविषयाध्यवसायो दृष्टं त्रिविधमनुमानमाख्यातम् ।
तल्लिङ्गलिङ्गपूर्वकमाप्तश्रुतिराप्तवचनं   तु   ॥ ५ ॥

*Prativishayaadhyavasaayo   drishtam   trividhamanumaana-
maakhyaatam;
Tallingalingipoorvakamaaptashrutiraaptavachanam tu.* (5)

Direct experience or perception is the reflective discerning
(adhyavasaya) of each object *(vishaya)* by the senses. Inference
is three-fold and is based on knowledge of the middle term
(linga) and a major term *(lingin)*. Valid testimony is due to
trustworthy or competent persons and the Vedas.

सामान्यतस्तु दृष्टादतीन्द्रियाणां प्रतीतिरनुमानात् ।
तस्मादपि   चासिद्धं   परोक्षमाप्तागमात्सिद्धम् ॥ 6 ॥

*Saamaanyatastu drishtaadateendriyaanaam prateetiranumaanaat;
Tasmaadapi chaasiddham parokshamaaptaagamaatsiddham.* (6)

Generally, ordinary knowledge is through perception.
Cognition that transcends the sense capabilities is established
through inference. What cannot be known through inference
is established through statements of reliable persons and
reliable scripture *(aptagama)*.

अतिदूरात्सामीप्यादिदिन्द्रियघातान्मनोऽनवस्थानात् ।
सौक्ष्म्यात्   व्यवधानाभिभवात्समानाभिहाराच्च ॥ 7 ॥

*Atidooraatsaameepyaadindriyaghaataanmano'navasthaanaat;
Saukshmyaat vyavadhaanaabhibhavaatsamaanaabhihaaraachcha.* (7)

Correct apprehension may not arise due to: great distance,
proximity, incorrect functioning or impairment of the senses,
absent-mindedness, great subtlety, being hidden, suppression
by something else (e.g. something overcome by darkness or
brightness), intermixture or confusion with similar things
(e.g. a grain of rice in a heap of rice).

सौक्ष्म्यातदनुपलब्धिर्नाभावात्कार्यतस्तदुपलब्धे: ।
महदादि तच्च कार्यं प्रकृतिसरूपं विरूपं च ॥ 8 ॥

Saukshmyaatadanupalabdhirnaabhaavaatkaaryatastadupalabdheh;
Mahadaadi tachcha kaaryam prakritisaroopam viroopam cha. (8)

Prakriti (the creative force) is not cognized because of its subtlety; not due to its non-existence. It can be known from its effects, namely mahat (supreme intelligence) and the others. These evolutes are both similar to, and different in form from, Prakriti.

असदकरणादुपादानग्रहणात   सर्वसंभवाभावात् ।
शक्तस्य शक्यकरणात् कारणभावाच्च सत् कार्यम् ॥ 9 ॥

Asadakaranaadupaadaanagrahanaat sarvasambhavaabhaavaat;
Shaktasya shakyakaranaat kaaranabhaavaachcha sat kaaryam. (9)

An effect *(karya)* pre-exists or resides *(satkarya)* in its cause in a potential state or condition prior to the operation of the cause since: something cannot arise from nothing; effects require adequate material causes *(upadana)*; all effects cannot arise from all causes *(sarvasambhavabhavat)*; an efficient cause can only produce that for which it is efficient (*shaktasya shakyakaranat*); an effect is of the same essence as its cause.

हेतुमदनित्यमव्यापि सक्रियमनेकमाश्रितं लिङ्गम् ।
सावयवं   परतन्त्रं   व्यक्तं   विपरीतमव्यक्तम् ॥ 10 ॥

Hetumadanityamavyaapi sakriyamanekamaashritam lingam;
Saavayavam paratantram vyaktam vipareetamavyaktam. (10)

Manifest *(vyakta)* creation has a cause *(hetumat)*, is impermanent *(anitya)*, is non-pervasive *(avyapin)*, is active or mobile *(sakriya)*, is multiple or multiform *(aneka)*, is dependent or supported *(ashrita)*, is a mark (for inference regarding Prakriti) or is mergent *(linga)*, is made up of parts *(savayava)*, and is subordinate (*paratantra*). The unmanifest (*avyakta*) is the reverse of this.

त्रिगुणमविवेकि विषय: सामान्यमचेतनं प्रसवधर्मि ।
व्यक्तं तथा प्रधानं तद्विपरीतस्तथा च पुमान् ॥ ११ ॥

Trigunamaviveki vishayah saamaanyamachetanam prasavadharmi;
Vyaktam tathaa pradhaanam tadvipareetastathaa cha pumaan. (11)

Both the manifest (vyakta) and the unmanifest (avyakta) *Pradhana* (Prakriti as the primal cause), consist of the three constituents (*triguna: sattwa, rajas* and *tamas*), are indistinguishable in an ultimate sense (*avivekin*), are objective (*vishaya*), are general (*samanya*), are non-conscious (*achetana*), and are prolific or productive (*prasavadharmin*). Purusha, the spirit, has the reverse of these characteristics of the manifest and unmanifest, yet it is similar to them in some respects.

प्रीत्यप्रीतिविषादात्मका: प्रकाशप्रवृत्तिनियमार्था: ।
अन्योन्याभिभवाश्रयजननमिथुनवृत्तयश्च गुणा: ॥ १२ ॥

Preetyapreetivishaadaatmakaah prakaashapravrittiniyamaarthaah;
Anyonyaabhibhavaashrayajananamithunavrittayashcha gunah. (12)

The three constituent processes (*gunas*) are experienced as contentment (*preeti*), discontent (*apreeti*) and depression or delusion (*vishada*). Their purpose is to illumine (*prakasha*), to activate (*pravritti*) and to restrain (*niyama*) respectively. They are mutually dominating, supporting, productive and cooperative.

सत्त्वं लघु प्रकाशकमिष्टमुपष्टम्भकं चलं च रज: ।
गुरु वरणकमेव तम: प्रदीपवच्चार्थतो वृत्ति: ॥ १३ ॥

Sattvam laghu prakaashakamishtamupashthambhakam chalam cha rajah;
Guru varanakameva tamah pradeepavachchaarthato vrttih. (13)

99

Sattwa is light or buoyant *(laghu)* and illuminating *(prakasha)*.
Rajas promotes desire and is stimulating *(upashthambhaka)*
and mobile *(chala)*. Tamas is heavy or sluggish *(guru)* and
obscuring or enveloping *(varanaka)*. They function for a single
purpose like the components of a lamp, whose purpose is
illumination.

अविवेक्यादेस्सिद्धिस्त्रैगुण्यात्तद्विपर्ययाभावात् ।
कारणगुणात्मकत्वात्कार्यस्याव्यक्तमपि सिद्धम् ॥ 14 ॥

Avivekyaadesiddhistraigunyaattadviparyayaabhaavaat;
Kaaranagunaatmakatvaatkaaryasyaavyaktamapi siddham. (14)

The existence of indistinguishability, etc. (in the manifest
and the unmanifest) (verse 11) is proved from their being
constituted of three gunas and from the absence of their
reverse. The existence of the unmanifest is proved from the
effects possessing the attributes of the cause.

भेदानां परिमाणात्, समन्वयात् शक्तित: प्रवृत्तेश्च ।
कारणकार्यविभागादविभागाद्वैश्वरूप्यस्य   ॥ 15 ॥

Bhedaanaam parimaanaat, samanvayaat shaktitah pravritteshcha;
Kaaranakaaryavibhaagaadavibhaagaadvaishvaroopyasya. (15)

The unmanifest is the ultimate cause because of: the finite
(limited) nature of specific objects of the evolutes *(bhedanam
parimanat)*; all manifest objects have uniform and homogenous
attributes *(samanvaya)*, hence they presuppose an efficient or
potent cause *(shakti karana)* that initiates the process;
differentiation between cause and effect *(karanakaryavibhagat)*;
and then non-differentiation or merging of the whole world
of effects *(avibhagadvaishvaroopyasya)*.

कारणमस्त्यव्यक्तं प्रवर्तते त्रिगुण: समुदयाच्च ।
परिणामत: सलिलवत् प्रतिप्रतिगुणाश्रयविशेषात् ॥ 16 ॥

Kaaranamastyavyaktam pravartate trigunatah samudayaachchha;
Parinaamatah salilavat pratipratigunaaashrayavisheshaat. (16)

The unmanifest operates through the three constituents (guna) by combination and modification; the three gunas together constitute its very nature *(trigunatmika)*; they continually undergo transformations which can be understood from the individual characteristics of the guna *(prati-pratigunashrayavisheshat)*, like water assuming tastes such as sweet, sour, etc., although itself tasteless.

सङ्घातपरार्थत्वात् त्रिगुणादिविपर्ययादधिष्ठानात् ।
पुरुषोऽस्ति भोक्तृभावात् कैवल्यार्थ प्रवृत्तेश्च ॥ 17 ॥

Sanghaataparaarthatvaat trigunaadiviparyayaadadhishthaanaat;
Purusho'sti bhoktribhaavaat kaivalyaartha pravritteshcha. (17)

Consciousness (Purusha) exists because: all aggregates exist for the purpose of something else *(sanghat pararthatvat)*; the unmanifest and manifest are both aggregates (made up of the gunas) (verses 14–16) hence the 'something else' must be distinct from 'the unmanifest and manifest' by not having the three attributes *(trigunadi viparyayat)*; there must be some controller or basis *(adhishthana)* of the unmanifest and manifest; this 'something else' must also be the basis of subjective experience *(bhoktribhava)*; and lastly, there is universal striving after freedom or isolation *(kaivalya)*.

जन्ममरणकरणानां प्रतिनियमादयुगपत्प्रवृत्तेश्च ।
पुरुषबहुत्वं सिद्धं त्रैगुण्यविपर्ययाच्चैव ॥ 18 ॥

Janmamaranakaranaanaam pratiniyamaadayugapatpravritteshcha;
Purushabahutvam siddham traigunyaviparyayaachchaiva. (18)

The multiplicity of Purusha *(purusha bahutvam)* is established from: the varieties of births, lives and deaths and functional capabilities of individuals; the non-simultaneity of these activities; the diverse modifications of the three gunas.

तस्माच्च विपर्यासात् सिद्धं साक्षित्वमस्य पुरुषस्य ।
कैवल्यं   माध्यस्थ्यं   द्रष्ट्टत्वमकर्तृभावश्च ॥ 19 ॥

Tasmaachcha viparyaasaat siddham saakshitvamasya purushasya;
Kaivalyam maadhyasthyam drashttatvamakartribhaavashcha. (19)

Because pure consciousness (Purusha) is the opposite of that
which consists of the three gunas, it follows that: it is the
pure witness *(sakshitva),* it is solitary *(kaivalya),* it is neutral
(separate from specific experience) *(madhyasthya),* and it is
not an agent *(akartribhava).*

तस्मात्तत्संयोगादचेतनं चेतनावदिव लिङ्गम् ।
गुणकर्तृत्वेऽपि तथा   कर्तेव   भवत्युदासीनः ॥ 20 ॥

Tasmaattatsamyogaadachetanam chetanaavadiva lingam;
Gunakartritve'pi tathaa karteva bhavatyudaaseenah. (20)

Because of the conjunction *(samyoga)* with Purusha, the
insentient evolute *(achetana lingam)* of Prakriti appears to
have consciousness. Similarly the neutral consciousness
appears to have agency, though all agency is solely due to the
three constituent gunas.

पुरुषस्य दर्शनार्थं कैवल्यार्थं तथा प्रधानस्य ।
पङ्ग्वन्धवदुभयोरपि   संयोगस्तत्कृतः   सर्गः ॥ 21 ॥

Purushasya darshanaartham kaivalyaartham tathaa pradhaanasya;
Pangvandhavadubhayorapi samyogastatkritah sargah. (21)

For revealing the entire dimension of Prakriti to Purusha,
and for liberation *(kaivalyartham)* of Prakriti, there is
conjunction or association (samyoga) between Purusha and
Prakriti like the cooperation between the lame and the blind.
From this association proceeds creation or manifestation.

प्रकृतेर्महांस्ततोऽहङ्कारस्तस्माद्गणश्च षोडशक: ।
तस्मादपि षोडशकात्पञ्चभ्य: पञ्च भूतानि ॥ 22 ॥

Prakritermahaamstato'hankaarastasmaadganashcha shodashakah;
Tasmaadapi shodashakaatpanchabhyah pancha bhootaani. (22)

From Prakriti arises mahat, from this evolves ahamkara and from this the group of sixteen (namely manas, the five sense capacities known as jnanendriya or buddhi-indriya; the five action capacities, karmendriya, and the five subtle elements, tanmatra). The five gross elements, known as bhoota or mahabhoota, arise from five of this sixteen (namely from the five subtle elements).

अध्यवसायो बुद्धिधर्मो ज्ञानं विराग ऐश्वर्यम् ।
सात्त्विकमेतद्रूपं तामसमस्माद्विपर्य्यस्तम् ॥ 23 ॥

Adhyavasaayo buddhidharmo jnaanam viraaga aishvaryam;
Saattvikametadroopam taamasamasmaadviparyyastam. (23)

Buddhi, also known as *mahat* (intellect, intuition) is characterized by will and reflective discerning *(adhavasaya)*. Its sattwic nature has four forms *(roopa)*: appropriate behaviour *(dharma)*, discriminative knowledge *(jnana)*, non-attachment *(viraga)*, and auspicious attainments and perfection *(aishwarya)*. Its tamasic forms are opposite to these in nature.

अभिमानोऽहंकार: तस्माद् द्विविध: प्रवर्तते सर्ग: ।
एकादशकश्च गण: तन्मात्रपञ्चकश्चैव ॥ 24 ॥

Abhimaano'hankaarah tasmaad dvividhah pravartate sargah;
Ekaadashakashcha ganah tanmaatrapanchakashchaiva. (24)

Ahamkara, or egoism, is characterized by self-assertion *(abhimana)* and gives rise to a two-fold evolution, namely the group of eleven (manas, five jnanendriya and five karmendriya), and the five-fold primary or subtle elements *(tanmatra)*.

103

सात्त्विक एकादशकः प्रवर्तते वैकृतादहङ्कारात् ।
भूतादेस्तन्मात्रः   स   तामसस्तैजसादुभयम् ॥ 25 ॥

Saattvika ekaadashakah pravartate vaikritaadahamkaaraat;
Bhootaadestanmaatrah sa taamasastaijasaadubhayam. (25)

The group of eleven, which is sattwic in nature, emerges out
of sattwic ahamkara *(vaikrita)*. The five tanmatras emerge
from tamasic ahamkara *(bhootadi)*. Both groups manifest due
to the influence of rajas on ahamkara *(taijasadubhayam)*.

बुद्धीन्द्रियाणि चक्षुः श्रोत्रघ्राणरसनत्वगाख्यानि   ।
वाक्पाणिपादपायूपस्थाः   कर्मेन्द्रियाण्याहुः ॥ 26 ॥

Buddhi-indryaani chakshuh shrotraghraanarasanatvagaakhyaani;
Vaakpaanipaadapaayoopasthah karmendriyaanyaahuh. (26)

Buddhi-indriya or *jnanendriya (the sense capabilities)* are:
seeing *(chakshu)*, hearing *(shrotra)*, smelling *(ghrana)*, tasting
(rasa), and touching *(tvak)*. *Karmendriya (the capabilities for*
action) are: speaking *(vak)*, grasping or handling *(pani)*,
walking or locomotion *(pada)*, excretion or expelling of waste
(payu), and sexual procreation or interaction *(upastha)*.

उभयात्मकमत्र मनः, संकल्पकमिन्द्रियं च साधर्म्यात् ।
गुणपरिणामविशेषान्नानात्वं   बाह्यभेदाश्च ॥ 27 ॥

Ubhayaatmakamatra manah, sankalpakamindriyan cha saadharmyaat;
Gunaparinaamavisheshaannaanaatvam baahyabhedaashcha. (27)

Manas possesses the nature of both (the sensory and motor
capabilities). It is the deliberating principle *(sankalpaka)* and
also a sense organ since it possesses properties common to
the sense organs. The multifariousness *(nanatvam)* and the
external diversities (of things apprehended by the mind)
arise due to the specific transformations of the gunas *(guna*
parinama visheshat).

रूपादिषु पञ्चानाम् आलोचनमात्रमिष्यते वृत्ति: ।
वचनादानविहरणोत्सर्गानन्दश्च   पञ्चानाम् ॥ 28 ॥

Roopaadishu panchaanaam aalochanamaatramishyate vrittih;
Vachanaadaanaviharanotsargaanandashcha panchaanaam. (28)

The function of the five sense capabilities of form (*rupa*) and
others is mere observation (*alochanamatra*) of sound, etc.
The functions of the five action capabilities are speech,
manipulation, locomotion, excretion and gratification.

स्वालक्षण्यं वृत्तिस्त्रयस्य सैषा भवत्यसामान्या।
सामान्यकरणवृत्ति: प्राणाद्या वायव: पञ्च ॥ 29 ॥

Svaalakshanyam vrittistrayasya saishaa bhavatyasaamaanyaa;
Saamaanyakaranavrittih praanaadhyaa vaayavah pancha. (29)

Mahat, ahamkara and manas have specific and distinguishable
functions, namely, *adhyavasaya* (reflective discernment),
abhimana (self-assertion) and the process of deliberation or
thought and analysis (*sankalpa*) (verses 23, 24 and 27). The
common function of this triad is to support or maintain the
vital airs (*prana* etc.) i.e. the maintenance of life.

युगपच्चतुष्टयस्य तु वृत्ति: क्रमशश्च तस्य निर्दिष्टा ।
दृष्टे तथाप्यदृष्टे त्रयस्य तत्पूर्विका वृत्ति: ॥ 30 ॥

Yugapachchatushtayasya tu vrittih kramashashcha tasya nirdishtaa;
Drishte tathaapyadrishte trayasya tatpoorvikaa vrittih. (30)

The functioning of this group of four (mahat, ahamkara and
manas and one of the senses) is either simultaneous or
successive with regard to the perceived objects. Similarly
when awareness arises of something not perceived (e.g.
conceptualization, logical inference, etc.), the three (mahat,
ahamkara and manas) work on the basis of what has been
previously perceived (and retained in memory, imagination
etc.). This is true for perceived objects also.

स्वां स्वां प्रतिपद्यन्ते परस्पराकूतहेतुकां वृत्तिम् ।
पुरुषार्थ एव हेतुर्न केनचित्कार्यते करणम् ॥ 31 ॥

Svaam svaam pratipadyante parasparaakootahetukaam vrittim;
Purushaartha eva heturna kenachitkaaryate karanam. (31)

These function and enter into their respective modifications
being incited by mutual impulse. The purpose of Purusha
(purushartha) is the only motive for their activities. They
never function for any other purpose.

करणं त्रयोदशविधम् तदाहरणधारणप्रकाशकरम् ।
कार्यं च तस्य दशधाऽऽहार्यं धार्यं प्रकाश्यं च ॥ 32 ॥

Karanam trayodashavidham tadaaharanadhaaranaprakaashakaram;
Kaaryam cha tasya dashadhaa'haaryam dhaaryam prakaashyam
cha. (32)

The thirteen-fold instrument (mahat, ahamkara, manas, five
karmendriyas and five jnanendriyas) is the basis of seizing
(aharana), holding or sustaining *(dharana)* and illuminating
(prakasha). The objects that are seized, held and illuminated
are of ten kinds.

अन्त:करणं त्रिविधं दशधा बाह्यम् त्रयस्य विषयाख्यम् ।
साम्प्रतकालं बाह्यं त्रिकालमाभ्यन्तरं करणम् ॥ 33 ॥

Antahkaranam trividham dashadhaa baahyam trayasya
vishayaakhyam;
Saampratakaalam baahyam trikaalamaabhyantaram karanam. (33)

The internal instrument *(antahkarana)* is threefold, and the
external *(bahya* or *bahirkarana)* is tenfold providing the sense
contents *(vishaya)* of experience. The external instruments
function in the present and the internal instruments function
in all three times *(trikala)*.

बुद्धीन्द्रियाणि तेषां पञ्च विशेषाविशेषविषयाणि ।
वाग्भवति शब्दविषया शेषाणि तु पञ्चविषयाणि ॥ 34 ॥

Buddhi-indriyani teshaam pancha visheshaavisheshavishayaani;
Vaagbhavati shabdavishayaa sheshaani tu panchavishayaani. (34)

The sense contents of the five sense capabilities are both
specific or gross *(vishesa)* and non-specific, general or subtle
(avishesa). The speech capability has only sound as content,
but the other four action capacities have contents of all five
kinds of sensing.

सान्तःकरणा बुद्धिः सर्वं विषयमवगाहते यस्मात् ।
तस्मात् त्रिविधं ॅ हरणं द्वारि द्वाराणि शेषाणि ॥ 35 ॥

Saantahkaranaa buddhih sarvam vishayamavagaahate yasmaat;
Tasmaat trividham karanam dvaari dvaaraani sheshaani. (35)

Because the supreme intelligence (mahat or buddhi) together
with the other internal instruments comprehends the entire
field of objects, the three-fold internal instrument can be
called the door-keeper *(dvarin)* and the ten-fold external
ones are the doors *(dvara)*.

एते प्रदीपकल्पाः परस्परविलक्षणा गुणविशेषाः ।
कृत्स्नं पुरुषस्यार्थं प्रकाश्य बुद्धौ प्रयच्छति ॥ 36 ॥

Ete pradeepakalpaah parasparavilakshanaa gunavisheshaah;
Kritsnam purushasyaartham prakaashya buddhau prayachchhati.
(36)

These (the group of thirteen: ahamkara, manas and the ten
sense and action capabilities) have their own characteristic
differences due to the differing modifications of the attributes
(gunavishesha). They function together, like the components
of a lamp, illuminating all the field of experience and
presenting it to the supreme intelligence (buddhi) for the

107

purposes of Purusha (namely, experience and subsequent liberation).

सर्वं प्रत्युपभोगं यस्मात्पुरुषस्य साधयति बुद्धि: ।
सैव च विशिनष्टि पुन: प्रधानपुरुषान्तरं सूक्ष्मम् ॥ 37 ॥

*Sarvam pratyupabhogam yasmaatpurushashya saadhayati buddhih;
Saiva cha vishinashti punah pradhaanapurushaantaram
sookshmam.* (37)

Because buddhi accomplishes presenting the experiences of all objects to Purusha, it additionally discriminates the subtle difference between Prakriti (Pradhana) and Purusha .

तन्मात्राण्यविशेषास्तेभ्यो भूतानि पञ्च पञ्चभ्य: ।
एते स्मृता विशेषा: शान्ता घोराश्च मूढाश्च ॥ 38 ॥

*Tanmaatraanyavisheshaastebhyo bhootaani pancha panchabhyah;
Ete smritaa visheshaah shaantaa ghoraashcha moodhaashcha.* (38)

The subtle elements (tanmatra) are non-specific or subtle (avishesha). The five gross elements (bhoota or mahabhoota) arise from the five subtle elements and are specific (vishesha) and are experienced as calm *(shanta)*, turbulent or uncomfortable *(ghora)* and faint, deluding or confusing *(moodha)*.

सूक्ष्मा: मातापितृजा: सह प्रभूतै: त्रिधा विशेषा: स्यु: ।
सूक्ष्मास्तेषाम् नियता मातापितृजा निवर्तन्ते ॥ 39 ॥

*Sookshmaah maataapitrijaah saha prabhutaih tridhaa visheshaah syuh;
Sookshmaasteshaam niyataa maataapitrijaa nivartante.* (39)

The subtle *(sukshma)* body, and the body born of mother and father *(matapitrija)*, together with the objects made of the gross elements *(prabhoota)*, are specific. Of these, the subtle

body is constant, and continues to exist from one life to the
next, whereas the gross body born of parents perishes.

पूर्वोत्पन्नमसक्तं नियतं महदादि सूक्ष्मपर्यन्तम् ।
संसरति निरुपभोगं भावैरधिवासितं लिङ्गम् ॥ ४० ॥

*Poorvotpannamasaktam niyatam mahadaadi sookshmaparyantam;
Samsarati nirupabhogam bhaavairadhivaasitam lingam.* (40)

The mergent or subtle vehicle *(lingam)* pre-exists all other
bodies *(purvotpanna)*, is unattached or unconfined *(asakta)*, is
constant or persistent *(niyata)*, and is composed of tattwas
beginning with mahat and ending with tanmatras (intellect,
ego, mind, ten capabilities and the five subtle elements). It is
free or devoid of experience, transmigrates or reincarnates
and is tinted or scented by the basic predispositions *(bhava)*.

चित्रं यथाश्रयमृते स्थाण्वादिभ्यो विना यथा छाया ।
तद्वद्विना विशेषैर्न तिष्ठति निराश्रयं लिङ्गम् ॥ ४१ ॥

*Chitram yathaasrayamrite sthaanvaadibhyo vinaa yathaa chaayaa;
Tadvadvinaa visheshairna tishthati niraashrayam lingam.* (41)

Just as a painting cannot exist without a support (canvas) or
as a shadow cannot exist without a stake or post, the subtle
body (or the mergent lingam) cannot exist without an
appropriate support.

पुरुषार्थहेतुकमिदं निमित्तनैमित्तिक प्रसङ्गेन ।
प्रकृतेर्विभुत्व योगान्नटवद्व्यवतिष्ठते लिङ्गम् ॥ ४२ ॥

*Purushaarthahetukamidam nimittanaimittika prasangena;
Prakritervibhutva yogaannatavadvyavatishthate lingam.* (42)

The subtle body, motivated by the purpose of consciousness
(Purusha), appears in different roles like a dramatic actor,
and functions by means of the efficient causes and effects

(nimittanaimittika) originating from the inherent power of manifest nature (Prakriti).

सांसिद्धिकाश्च भावा: प्राकृतिका वैकृतिकाश्च धर्माद्या: ।
दृष्टा: करणाश्रयिण: कार्याश्रयिणश्च कललाद्या: ॥ 43 ॥

Saamsiddhikaashcha bhaavaah praakritikaa vaikritikaashcha dharmaadyaah;
Drishtaah karanaashrayinah kaaryaashrayinashcha kalalaadyaah. (43)

The innate *(samsiddhika)* predispositions *(bhava)*, starting with virtuous nature or appropriate behaviour *(dharma)*, are natural *(prakritika)* or acquired *(vaikritika)*. These predispositions inhere in buddhi (verse 23), embryo and the body.

धर्मेण गमनमूर्ध्वं गमनमधस्ताद्भवत्यधर्मेण ।
ज्ञानेन चापवर्गो विपर्ययादिष्यते बन्ध: ॥ 44 ॥

Dharmena gamanamoordhvam gamanamadhastaadbhavatya-dharmena;
Jnaanena chaapavargo viparyayaadishyate bandhah. (44)

Through the predisposition towards virtuous nature *(dharma)* one ascends to higher planes of existence; through inappropriate or vicious behaviour *(adharma)* one descends to lower planes. Through knowledge comes release and by its reverse (i.e. *avidya* or ignorance) one becomes bound.

वैराग्यात्प्रकृतिलय: संसारो भवति राजसाद्रागात् ।
ऐश्वर्यादविघातो विपर्ययात्तद्विपर्यास: ॥ 45 ॥

Vairaagyaatprakritilayah samsaaro bhavati raajasaadraagaat;
Aishvaryaadavighaato viparyayaattadviparyaasah. (45)

From the predisposition towards non-attachment *(vairagya)* (but continuing ignorance of Purusha), results absorption into Prakriti; from rajasic passionate attachment *(raga)* one transmigrates; from power one attains removal of obstacles or control over one's life, from its reverse one loses control of life.

एष प्रत्ययसर्गो विपर्ययाऽशक्तितुष्टिसिद्ध्याख्यः ।
गुणवैषम्यविम-त्तिस्य च भेदास्तु पञ्चाशत् ॥ ४६॥

Esha pratyayasargo viparyayaa'shaktitushtisiddhyaakhyah;
Gunavaishamyavimarddaattasya cha bhedaastu panchaashat. (46)

This (evolution of the dispositions) is the creation of buddhi *(pratyayasarga)*, has fifty divisions and manifests in four general classes: ignorance, misconception or wrong belief *(viparyaya)*; incompetence or dysfunctionality *(ashakti)*; contentment *(tushti)*; and perfection or attainments *(siddhi)*. This evolution is due to the unequal mutual impact of the three attributes (guna).

पञ्चविपर्ययभेदाः भवन्त्यशक्तिश्च करणवैकल्यात् ।
अष्टाविंशतिभेदा तुष्टिर्नवधाऽष्टधा सिद्धिः ॥ ४७॥

Panchaviparyayabhedaah bhavantyashaktishcha karanavaikalyaat;
Ashthaavimshatibhedaa tushtirnavadhaa'shtadhaa siddhih. (47)

There are five kinds of wrong belief (viparyaya); twenty-eight kinds of dysfunction caused by defects in one's capabilities (ashakti); nine kinds of contentment (tushti) and eight perfections (siddhi).[1]

भेदस्तमसोऽष्टविधो मोहस्य च दशविधो महामोहः ।
तामिस्रोऽष्टादशधा तथा भवत्यन्धतामिस्रः ॥ ४८॥

---

[1] In Patanjali's *Yoga Sutras*, false belief or ignorance is differentiated into nescience *(avidya)*, ego *(asmita)*, attachment *(raga)*, aversion *(dwesha)* and clinging *(abhinivesha)*. Here they are respectively known as obscurity *(tamas)*, delusion *(moha)*, extreme delusion *(mahamoha)*, gloom *(tamisra)* and blinding gloom *(andhatamisra)*.

Bhedastamaso'shtavidho mohasya cha dashavidho mahaamohah;
Taamisro'shtaadashadhaa tathaa bhavatyandhataamisrah. (48)

There are eight varieties of darkness *(tamas)* and also of delusion *(moha)*, ten kinds of extreme delusion *(mahamoha)*, and eighteen varieties each of gloom *(tamisra)* and blinding gloom *(andhatamisra)*.

एकादशेन्द्रियवधाः सह बुद्धिवधैरशक्तिरुि-ष्टा ।
सप्तदशावधा बुद्धेर्विपर्ययात्तुष्टिसिद्धीनाम् ॥ 49 ॥

Ekaadashendriyavadhaah saha buddhivadhairashaktiruddishtaa;
Saptadashavadhaa buddherviparyayaattushtisiddheenaam. (49)

The dysfunctions include injuries to the eleven capabilities (manas and the ten indriya) as well as seventeen kinds of injuries to the intellect (buddhi) which correspond to the reverse of the nine contentments and eight perfections.

आध्यात्मिक्यश्चतस्रः प्रकृत्युपादानकाल भाग्याख्याः ।
बाह्या विषयोपरमात्पञ्च च नव तुष्टयोऽभिमताः ॥ 50 ॥

Aadhyaatmikyashchatasrah prakrityupaadaanakaala bhaagyaakhyaah;
Baahyaa vishayoparamaatpancha cha nava tushtayo'bhimataah. (50)

The nine kinds of contentment have a two-fold classification as four internal ones, including belief in primordial matter or nature as ultimate, belief in a material basis *(upadana)* as ultimate, belief in time *(kala)* as ultimate, and belief in providence *(bhagya)* as ultimate; and five external ones, due to turning away from the objects of the five sense capabilities.

ऊहः शब्दोऽध्ययनं दुःखविघातास्त्रयः सुहृत्प्राप्तिः ।
दानं च सिद्धयोऽष्टौ सिद्धेः पूर्वोऽङ्कुशः त्रिविधः ॥ 51 ॥

Oohah shabdo'dhyayanam duhkhavighaataastrayah suhritpraaptih;
Daanam cha siddhayo'shtau siddheh poorvo'nkushah trividhah. (51)

The eight attainments (siddhi) are reflective reasoning (*oohah*), oral instruction (shabdah), study (adhyayanam), the three-fold destruction of suffering (dukhavighatastrayah) (verse 1), companionship with well-wishers *(suhritpraptih)*, and giving nature *(danam)*. The three that precede attainments (namely, misconceptions, dysfunctions and contentments) are obstacles to the attainments.

न विना भावैर्लिङ्गं न लिङ्गेन भावनिर्वृत्ति: ।
लिङ्गाख्यो भावाख्यस्तस्माद्द्वेधा प्रवर्तते सर्ग: ॥ 52 ॥

Na vinaa bhaavairlingam na lingena bhaavanirvrittih;
Lingaakhyo bhaavaakhyastasmaaddvedhaa pravartate sargah. (52)

The subtle nature cannot evolve without the predispositions (bhava), and without the subtle nature (lingam) the pre-dispositions are inoperative. Therefore, evolution proceeds in two ways *(dvividhasarga)* as the objective and subjective respectively called 'subtle creation' and 'predisposition creation'.

अष्टविकल्पो दैवस्तैर्यग्योनश्च पञ्चधा भवति ।
मानुषक श्चैकविध: समासतो भौतिक: सर्ग: ॥ 53 ॥

Ashthavikalpo daivastairyagyonashcha panchadhaa bhavati;
Maanushaka schaikavidhah samaasato bhautikah sargah. (53)

Celestials (*daiva*) consist of eight varieties; the lower beings *(tairyagyona)* are of five varieties; and humans *(manusha)* are of one kind. This, in brief, is the elemental or material creation (*bhautika sarga*).

ऊर्ध्वं सत्त्वविशालस्तमोविशालश्च मूलत: सर्ग: ।
मध्ये रजोविशालो ब्रह्मादिस्तम्बपर्यन्त: ॥ 54 ॥

Oordhvam sattvavishaalastamovishaalashcha moolatah sargah;
Madhye rajovishaalo brahmaadistambaparyantah. (54)

The higher regions abound in sattwa attribute; the lower regions abound in tamas attribute; and in the middle order rajas is preponderant. Such is the evolution of worlds from Brahma down to a blade of grass.

तत्र जरामरणकृतं दु:खं प्राप्नोति चेतन: पुरुष: ।
लिङ्गस्याविनिवृत्तेस्तस्मा-:खं   स्वभावेन ॥ 55 ॥

Tatra jaraamaranakritam duhkham praapnoti chetanah purushah; Lingasyaavinivrittestasmaadduhkham svabhaavena. (55)

Therein Purusha experiences suffering brought about by old age and death on account of non-cessation of the subtle body (*linga*). Therefore pain is the very nature of things.

इत्येष: प्रकृतिकृतो महदादिविशेषभूतपर्यन्त: ।
प्रतिपुरुषविमोक्षार्थं स्वार्थ इव परार्थ आरम्भ: ॥ 56 ॥

Ityeshah prakritikrito mahadaadivisheshabhootaparyantah; Pratipurushavimokshaartham svaartha iva paraartha aarambhah. (56)

Thus, this evolution caused by Prakriti, from mahat down to the gross elements (bhootas), operates for the sake of the final release of each separate self. It appears as if Prakriti were acting in her own interest, but in reality she acts in the interest of others.

वत्सविवृद्धिनिमित्तं क्षीरस्य यथा प्रवृत्तिरज्ञस्य ।
पुरुषविमोक्षनिमित्तं तथा प्रवृत्ति: प्रधानस्य ॥ 57 ॥

Vatsavivriddhinimittam ksheerasya yathaa pravrittirajnasya; Purushavimokshanimittam tathaa pravrittih pradhaanasya. (57)

Just as the secretion of milk, which is unintelligent, happens for the growth and nourishment of the calf, the action of the root cause (Pradhana) is for the sake of liberation of consciousness (Purusha).

औत्सुक्यनिवृत्यर्थं यथा क्रियासु प्रवर्तते लोक: ।
पुरुषस्य विमोक्षार्थं प्रवर्तते तद्वदव्यक्तम् ॥ 58 ॥

Autsukyanivrityartham yathaa kriyaasu pravartate lokah;
Purushasya vimokshaartham pravartate tadvadavyaktam. (58)

Even as people engage in activity to relieve desires, so also
the unmanifest Prakriti *(Avyakta)* functions for the sake of
emancipation of Purusha.

रङ्गस्य दर्शयित्वा निवर्तते नर्तकी यथा नृत्यात् ।
पुरुषस्य तथात्मानं प्रकाश्य विनिवर्त्तते प्रकृति: ॥ 59 ॥

Rangasya darshayitvaa nivartate narttakee yathaa nrityaat;
Purushasya tathaatmaanam prakaashya vinivarttate prakritih. (59)

Just as a dancing girl ceases to dance after being seen by the
audience, so Prakriti ceases to operate after having shown
herself to Purusha.

नानाविधैरुपायैरुपकारिण्यनुपकारिण: पुंस: ।
गुणवत्यगुणस्य सततस्तस्यार्थमपार्थकं चरति ॥ 60 ॥

Naanaavidhairupaayairupakaariniyanupakaarinah pumsah;
Gunavatyagunasya satastasyaarthamapaarthakam charati. (60)

Benevolent Prakriti, endowed with the (three) attributes
(gunas) aids consciousness in various ways without interests
of her own, and acts for the benefit of Purusha or the spirit
(pumsah) who is devoid of the attributes and confers no
benefit in return.

प्रकृते सुकुमारतरं न किञ्चिदस्तीति मे मतिर्भवति ।
या दृष्टास्मीति पुनर्दर्शनमुपैति पुरुषस्य ॥ 61 ॥

Prakrite sukumaarataram na kincidasteeti me matirbhavati;
Yaa drishtaa'smeeti punardarshanamupaiti purushasya. (61)

My opinion is that there is nothing more modest than *Prakriti*. Knowing 'I have been seen', she no longer comes within the sight of *Purusha*.

तस्मान्न बध्यतेऽसौ न मुच्यते नापि संसरति कश्चित् ।
संसरति बध्यते मुच्यते च नानाश्रया प्रकृतिः ॥ 62 ॥

Tasmaanna badhyate'sau na muchyate naapi samsarati kashchit;
Samsarati badhyate muchyate cha naanaashrayaa prakritih. (62)

Therefore, Purusha is never really bound, never liberated, nor does it transmigrate. It is only Prakriti who in her various manifestations, is bound, liberated and transmigrates.

रुपैः सप्तभिरेव तु बध्नात्यात्मानमात्मना प्रकृतिः ।
सैव च पुरुषार्थं प्रति विमोचयत्येकरूपेण ॥ 63 ॥

Roopaih saptabhireva tu badhnaatyaatmaanamaatmanaa prakritih;
Saiva cha purushaartham prati vimochayatyekaroopena. (63)

Prakriti herself binds herself, by herself, through the seven predispositions (verses 43–51). She again liberates herself by means of one form *(ekaroopa)* of disposition (namely, the predisposition for knowledge *(jnana))*, all for the sake of Purusha (Purushartha).

एवं तत्त्वाभ्यासान्नास्मि न मे नाहमित्यपरिशेषम् ।
अविपर्ययाद्विशुद्धं केवलमुत्पद्यते ज्ञानम् ॥ 64 ॥

Evam tattvaabhyaasaannaasmi na me naahamityaparishesham;
Aviparyayaadvishuddham kevalamutpadyate jnaanam. (64)

Thus from meditative analysis or discrimination *(abhyasa)* on the principles *(tattwa)* of Samkhya, discriminative knowledge *(jnana)* arises. It takes the form of "I am not", "Nothing is mine" and "Not I"; it is final or complete *(aparishesha)*, pure *(vishuddha)* due to being free from error *(aviparyaya)*, and is absolute knowledge *(kevala)*.

तेन   निवृत्तप्रसवार्थवशात्सप्तरूपविनिवृत्ताम् ।
प्रकृतिं परयति पुरुष: प्रेक्षकवदवस्थित: स्वच्छ: ॥ ६५ ॥

Tena nivrittaprasavaarthavashaatsaptaroopavinivrittaam;
Prakritim pashyati purushah prekshakavadavasthitah svachchah. (65)

Then Purusha, like a mere witness, beholds Prakriti, which has ceased from evolving products, and which has turned away from the seven forms of evolution, having served the purpose of Purusha.

दृष्टा मयेत्युपेक्षक एको दृष्टाहमित्युपरमत्यन्या ।
सति संयोगेऽपि तयो: प्रयोजनं नास्ति सर्गस्य ॥ ६६ ॥

Drishtaa mayetyupekshaka eko drishtaahamityuparamatyanyaa;
Sati samyoge'pi tayoh prayojanam naasti sargasya. (66)

The one witness, Purusha, thinks, "I have seen her". The other, Prakriti, thinks, "I have been seen" and ceases her activity. Though the association between them *(samyoga)* persists, there is no motive for further evolution.

सम्यग्ज्ञानाधिगमाद्धर्मादीनामकारणप्राप्तौ ।
तिष्ठति संस्कारवशाच्चक्रभ्रमिवद्धृतशरीर: ॥ ६७ ॥

Samyagjnaanaadhigamaaddharmaadeenaamakaaranapraaptau;
Tishthati samskaaravashaachchakrabhramivaddhritashareerah. (67)

Through the attainment of perfect, discriminating knowledge *(samyagjnana)*, dharma and the rest of the seven pre-dispositions become devoid of their causal efficacy. Yet, one continues to be invested with the body *(dhrita sharira)* due to the force of latent dispositions *(samskara)*, just like a potter's wheel continues to rotate due to the momentum transferred to it by the potter.

प्राप्ते शरीरभेदे चरितार्थत्वात्प्रधानविनिवृत्ते: ।
ऐकान्तिकमात्यन्तिकमुभयं कैवल्यमाप्नोति ॥ 68 ॥

Praapte shareerabhede charitaarthatvaatpradhaanavinivritteh;
Aikaantikamaatyantikamubhayam kaivalyamaapnoti. (68)

When separation from the gross body *(sharirabhede)* has taken place and Prakriti, as the root cause (Pradhana), ceases to operate, having accomplished the purpose of Purusha, Purusha attains liberation *(kaivalya)* that is both complete or absolute *(aikantika)* and final or permanent *(atyantika)*.

पुरुषार्थज्ञानमिदं गुह्यं परमर्षिणा समाख्यातम् ।
स्थित्युत्पत्तिप्रलयाश्चिन्त्यन्ते यत्र भूतानाम् ॥ 69 ॥

Purushaarthajnaanamidam guhyam paramarshinaa samaakhyaatam;
Sthityutpattipralayaashchintyante yatra bhootaanaam. (69)

This profound secret *(guhya)* knowledge for attaining the aim of Purusha has been expounded by the great sage *(rishi)*. In it, he has considered the duration *(sthiti)*, origin *(utpatti)* and ultimate dissolution *(pralaya)* of beings.

एतत्पवित्रमग्र्यं मुनिरासुरयेऽनुकम्पया प्रददौ ।
आसुरिरपि पञ्चशिखाय तेन बहुधा कृतं तन्त्रम ॥ 70 ॥

Etatpavitramagryam muniraasuraye'nukampayaa pradadau;
Aasurirapi panchashikhaaya tena bahudhaa kritam tantram. (70)

This foremost, pure and supreme doctrine, the sage (Kapila), moved by compassion, gave to Asuri. Asuri gave it to Panchashikha by whom the doctrine *(tantra)* was propounded extensively *(bahudha)*.

शिष्यपरम्परायाऽऽगतमीश्वरकृष्णेन चैतदार्याभिः ।
संक्षिप्तमार्यमतिना सम्यग्विज्ञाय सिद्धान्तम् ॥ 71 ॥

Shishyaparamparaayaa'gatameeshvarakrishnena chaitadaaryaabhih;
Samkshiptamaaryamatinaa samyagvijnaaya siddhaantam. (71)

This doctrine has been handed down through a succession
of teachers and pupils and has been condensed in the Arya
metre by the noble minded Ishvara Krishna, after having
been thoroughly understood by him.

सप्तत्यां किल येऽर्थास्तेऽर्थाः कृत्स्नस्य षष्टितन्त्रस्य ।
आख्यायिकाविरहिताः परवादविवर्जिताश्चापि ॥ 72 ॥

Saptatyaam kila ye'rthaaste'rthaah kritsnasya shashthitantrasya;
Aakhyaayikaavirahitaah paravaadavivarjitaashchaapi. (72)

The seventy verses include the meanings of the entire sixty
topics[2] *(shashtitantra)* of the traditional Samkhya, excluding
the anecdotes and polemic against its opponents.

---

[2] The sixty topics are:
1. *Pradhana* (14)
2. Her singleness, *ekatvam* (15)
3. Her objectiveness, *arthavattvam* (11)
4. Distinctness of Purusha and Prakriti, *athaanyatha* (11)
5. Her subordination to Purusha, *pararthyam* (17)
6. Plurality of Purusha, *anaikyam* (18)
7. Disconnection of Purusha from Prakriti at the end, *viyoga* (20)
8. Conjunction of Purusha and Prakriti in the beginning, *samyoga* (21)
9. Separateness of Purusha from specific experience, *Sheshavritti* (19)
10. Inactivity of Purusha, *akartribhava* (19)
These are 10 basic topics and in addition the following:
• Five kinds of error, *viparyaya* (47)
• Nine types of contentments, *tushti* (50)
• Twenty-eight types of dysfunctions, *karananam asamarthyam* (49)
• Eight forms of psychic powers, *siddhis* (51)

Glossary

Abhimana – self-assertion
Abhinivesha – fear of disconnection, fear of death
Achetana – absence of consciousness
Adhyavasaya – reflective discerning
Adhibhautika – conflict and pain which stems from the material world
Adhidaivika – conflict and pain which stems from cosmic influence
Adhishthanat – conscious guiding faculty
Adhyatmika – conflict and pain which stems from the personal inner experience
Adi – original
Adi Shankaracharya – original teacher of Advaita Vedanta who reorganized the sannyasa tradition and wrote commentaries on the major upanishads
Adishthana – fixed on its own axis
Adrishya – imperceptible
Advaita – Indian philosophy of non-dualism
Ahamkara – I-principle; ego-principle, individuating factor
Aharana – seizing
Aishwarya – auspicious attainments and perfection
Akarana – causeless
Akasha – space, ether
Akatribhava – non-agency
Ananda – bliss
Ananda samadhi – blissful absorption
Antahkarana – internal instrument
Anumana – inference

Aparinama – without consequences, eternally resultless

Apreeti – rejection, non-acceptance

Arjuna – devotee of Shri Krishna who received teachings on the battle-field of life as recorded in the *Bhagavad Gita*

Asadakaranat – proclamation of the theory of causation: if the existence of the effect is not true, then the cause cannot be the source of the effect

Asakta – unattached

Ashtanga yoga – the yoga of eight limbs, generally this refers to the raja yoga path outlined by Patanjali in the second chapter of the *Yoga Sutras*

Ashuddha tattwas – impure or mixed elements

Asmita samadhi – dissolution of ego

Atma – soul, spirit

Atriguna – beyond the three gunas

Atyantika – permanent

Avadharana – function of ascertainment

Avyayaya – partless one

Avidya – existence without recognition

Avishesha – non-specific evolute

Avyakta – unmanifest

Bahirkarana – external organs

Bhagavad Gita – part of the *Mahabharata* epic which records the ancient war instigated by Shri Krishna to re-establish dharma

Bhava – mood, attitude, predisposition

Bhokta – conscious enjoyer

Bhoktribhavat – subjective experience

Bhoota – see Mahabhoota

Brahma – state which evolves, which is responsible for evolution

Brahmi vritti – vritti which leads to transcendence

Buddhi – the supreme intelligence; see Mahat

Buddhi-indriyas – five sense capacities/organs of perception (see also Jnanendriyas)

Chaitanya – self-awareness

Chakshu – sense of sight, vision

Chala – mobile

Chetana – consciousness

Chit – consciousness

Darshana – philosophy; vision of truth

Dharana – concentration

Dharma – virtuous nature, appropriate behaviour

Dhyana – meditation

Deha buddhi – state of being in which the body still holds impressions which keep it together

Drashta – witness, which has knowledge but not the capacity to act; uninvolved observer, the onlooker; the consciousness which knows what is going on; the seer

Dravya – substance

Dukha – pain, aversion

Dukhatraya – three kinds of suffering

Duryodhana – chief of the demonic cousins of Arjuna and his opponent in the war recorded in the *Bhagavad Gita*

Dvaita – dualism

Dwesha – repulsion

Ekadhyana – awareness of one thing only

Ekanta – complete

Gaudapada Karika – commentary on *Samkhya Karika* written by Gaudapada

Ghrana – sense of smell

Guna – attribute; component of Prakriti

Gurukul – the school of the guru

Hiranyagarbha – womb of Prakriti

Iccha shakti – the force of pure desire or will

Indriyas – senses of perception and action

Indriya sanyam – managing the senses

Ishvara – the non-decaying Reality

Jada – insentient

Jada avastha – insentient state

Jivanmukti – state of consciousness where one is liberated in life

Jna – pure absolute knowledge

Jnana – knowledge

Jnana shakti – recognition, force of pure knowing

Jnanendriyas – organs of perception

Jnata – the knower

Jneya – which is known

Kaivalya – aloneness; freedom; beyond duality and Prakriti's clutches

Karana – cause

Karanabhavat – proclamation of the theory of causation: cause and effect are inseparable

Karmendriyas – organs of action
Kartavya – duty
Karya – effect
Karyakaran siddhanta – theory of causation
Karyakaranavada – theory of causation; see also Satkaryavada
Khya – understanding
Kriti – to perform, to do, to act
Kriya – motion
Kriya shakti – force of action, actualization
Laya – dissolution
Linga – symbol, mark
Linga sharira – subtle body
Mahabharata – great epic of ancient India
Mahabhootas – gross elements: space, air, fire, water, earth
Mahat – the great principle; the subtle and prominent cause for manifestation; see also Buddhi
Mahayana – the great path, an all-inclusive path of Buddhism
Manan – contemplation
Manas – process of thinking and analysis
Manas sanyam – managing the mind
Maya – that which limits or defines the area in which a form can manifest itself
Mimamsa – an orthodox school of India philosophy
Mithya – unreal, false
Moksha – liberation, freedom
Moola – base, root
Moola pradhana – original cause
Moola prakriti – basic form of Prakriti; the Unmanifest; the primordial energy
Mudra – attitude, gesture
Mukti – liberation
Murti – symbol, idol
Nidhidhyasana – sustained practice of meditation
Nidra – sleep
Nimitta karana – instrumental cause
Nirakara – formless
Nirishvaravada Samkhya – discussion on Samkhya without reference to God or with denial of the supreme Self
Nirvaiyaktika – impersonal
Nirnaya – the function of decision

Nishkriyata – inactivity, passivity
Nyaya – logic; an orthodox school of Indian philosophy
Pada – feet
Pancha – five
Pancha mahabhootas – the five gross elements
Pani – hands
Paramanu – subtle substance
Payu – excretory organs
Pra – prefix denoting intensity
Pradhana – main, primary cause
Prakasha – light
Prakriti – force of creation; vehicle of purusha
Pralaya – dissolution
Pramana – right relative knowledge
Prana – energy; vital force
Pratyahara – sense control; ability to turn the senses inward for introspection
Pratyaya – seed of karmas
Preeti – attraction or affection
Purusha – pure consciousness which sees and knows
Raga – attraction
Rajas – the quality of dynamism which binds one to the sufferings of samasara
Rasa – sense of taste
Roopa – form
Sah – with
Sakara – having a form
Sam – balanced
Sakshi – state of being the witness of the total
Samkhya – Indian dualistic philosophy; one of the six systems of vedic philosophy (darshanas), attributed to the sage Kapila.
Samkhya Karika – seventy-two sutras by Ishvara Krishna describing Samkhya as taught by Sage Kapila
Samkhya Pravachana Sutra – treatise by Sage Kapila about the basic concepts of Samkhya
Samsara – manifest world
Samya avastha – state in which all the gunas are balanced and in harmony
Samyaka jnana – the ultimate knowledge; right knowledge

Samyoga – combinations and permutations; association of Purusha and Prakriti

Sanghat – collection of objects which provide some benefit to the user

Sankalpa – will, resolve, act of deliberation

Sannyasa – total dedication, renunciation

Saroopa parinama – merging of a guna into itself

Sarvajnata – omniscient, all knowing

Sarvasambhavabhavat – proclamation of the theory of causation: a specific effect requires a specific cause (all effects cannot be produced from all causes)

Sat – truth; existence

Satkaryavada – theory of the existence of an effect in its cause

Sattwa – quality of knowledge and luminosity leading to liberation

Seshvara – with Ishvara or with God; it equals sah + Ishvara

Seshvaravada Samkhya – thoughts of Samkhya which accept God, the supreme Self, as the original source

Shaktasya-shakya-karanat – proclamation of the theory of causation: a desired effect can be attained only from a potent cause

Shakti – motion, continuous movement, power

Shakti karana – potent cause; the specific cause for a specific effect

Shankaracharya – see Adi Shankaracharya

Sharira – body (gross, subtle or causal)

Shashvata – eternal

Shiva – cosmic consciousness

Shivalingam – symbol of consciousness

Shwete – inactive, dormant

Shravana – sense of hearing

Shuddha chaitanya – pure awareness

Shuddha tattwas – pure elements

Siddhantavada – theory of evolution

Smriti – memory

Sparsha – sense of touch

Sthitaprajna – state of total witnessing; being established in knowing; a sage of steady wisdom described in the second chapter of the *Bhagavad Gita*

Sthiti – steady state

Sthoola sharira – gross body

Sukha – pleasure

Sukshma sharira – subtle body

Sutra – aphorism
Swatantra – independent principle
Swabhava – inherent nature
Tamas – quality of inertia, which veils the true nature of reality
Tanmatras – subtle elements
Tattwa – element
Tattva Samasa Pravachana Sutra – treatise by Sage Kapila about creation being the result of combinations and permutations of the tattwas
Triguna – composed of the three gunas
Trigunatita – beyond the three gunas
Trigunatmika – three gunas existing in total inactive equilibrium; three gunas existing together
Udasina – passivity; not being impressionable; indifference
Upadana – adequate material cause
Upadanagrahanat – proclamation of the theory of causation: before manifestation the effect is contained in the cause and it is part of the cause
Upastha – reproductive organs
Utpadan – actualization of the potential contained in the cause
Vada – discussion, thought, theory
Vairagya – non-attachment
Vaisheshika – one of the orthodox schools of Indian philosophy
Vak – speech
Vedanta – philosophy of the Upanishads
Videhamukti – state of liberation attained after death, where no karmas remain to necessitate rebirth
Vidya – recognition, knowledge of reality
Vishesha – specific evolute
Vikalpa – imagination
Viparyaya – false knowledge; misconception
Virupa parinama – merging of a guna into another guna
Vishada – indifference
Vishada Yoga – first chapter of the *Bhagavad Gita* – the yoga of depression
Viveka – wisdom, discrimination
Vyakta – manifest
Vyakta avastha – manifest state
Vyakta Prakriti – the manifest form of Prakriti
Yoga Sutras – system of raja yoga codified by Sage Patanjali